# The Problem of Study Guide

## A Bible Study on the C.S. Lewis Book
### *The Problem of Pain*

## By Alan Vermilye

"Pain insists upon being attended to. God whispers to us in our pleasures, speaks in our conscience, but shouts in our pain: it is His megaphone to rouse a deaf world." *The Problem of Pain*

**BROWN CHAIR BOOKS**
BOOKS THAT INSPIRE

# The Problem of Pain Study Guide
## A Bible Study on the C.S. Lewis Book
### *The Problem of Pain*

To learn more about this Bible study, to order additional copies, or to download the answer guide, visit **www.BrownChairBooks.com**.

Version 1

## ACKNOWLEDGMENTS

I would like to thank God for allowing me to experience pain.
How else could I otherwise relate to this book at all?

# TABLE OF CONTENTS

# INTRODUCTION

The world suffers in pain. We take every precaution to escape it, but it's unavoidable. The fact is, we will experience some degree of pain and suffering in our lives. I was 19 when my mother lost her battle with cancer. Any faith I possessed at that time was suddenly rocked at the thought of losing her. In fact, I was angry and had a lot of questions. Many of those questions I expressed to her in the last few weeks of her life. I struggled with reconciling how a wonderful Christian woman could be taken in the prime of her life, especially while others, whom I perceived as evil, flourished. What's the point? What benefit does it serve?

You, too, have experienced pain—the death of loved ones, the betrayal of those closest to you, the loss of a job, a child in rebellion, the diagnoses that you were not expecting, and the list goes on.

Most often our pain results in a one-word question: Why? The answer is that we live in a fallen and evil world. Although this may be the root cause, it does little to comfort the one who is suffering.

I often wonder if the problem of pain would be easier to manage if I were not a Christian. If there's no higher power who has the ability to resolve my pain, then my only refuge is to exhaust every possible worldly option until I succeed or give up in defeat. But then I remember that in defeat, there's no more hope.

As a believer, I have hope because I know God is all-powerful and will resolve my pain in His time. Unfortunately, our pain also brings a certain amount of impatience, which leaves us wondering: Where is God in all of this? Does He hear my cries for help? Does He even care? Why is He allowing such pain and misery in my life?

In *The Problem of Pain*, C.S. Lewis sums up the problem of pain like this: "If God is good and all-powerful, why does he allow his creatures to suffer pain?" As Christians seeking to sincerely follow God, this sounds like a fair question.

Lewis does not claim to offer a complete solution to the problem of pain but rather takes a philosophical approach. He makes it very clear in the preface that his main purpose for writing the book is "to solve the intellectual problem raised by suffering" and not "to teach fortitude and patience while suffering." So if you're trying to understand the grieving process, this is not the book or study for you. Later Lewis would take a more personal approach in a reflection on his own experiences of grief and anguish at the death of his wife in *A Grief Observed*.

What Lewis does offer is a very detailed and thought out explanation of God's ability to use pain for our good while never dismissing the fact that pain hurts. Pain is a reliable friend that keeps us humble and dependent on God, and when that friend departs, we often find ourselves returning to a life of self-sufficiency and sin.

Ultimately, Lewis challenges us to understand pain in the context of a God who provides meaning and hope in the person and work of Jesus Christ amid the pain. In His supreme act of self-surrender and love, He personally and profoundly experienced unjust pain and suffering to redeem our pain and suffering.

As His followers, we, too, are called to lives of submission and to walk as Jesus did. That walk will often include pain, although pain with a redemptive purpose. Perhaps as you have matured in your walk with Christ, you've been able to look back on your life and see how some of the worst experiences that you've had to endure have actually helped shape you into the person you are today.

As for my normal disclaimer, I'm not a biblical or Lewis scholar nor do I consider this study guide the most comprehensive work available on the book. However, it has helped me and many others come to a better understanding of this great Lewis classic. I hope it does for you as well.

# Course Notes and Study Format

**HOW TO USE THIS GUIDE**

*The Problem of Pain* by C.S. Lewis consists of a preface plus ten chapters. This study guide contains a study session for each chapter and can be used for individual study or as a group study gathering weekly to discuss each chapter.

**STUDYING**

You might find this book academic and difficult to read at times. I surely did, which is why I would suggest that each week you read one chapter all the way through. Then go back and reread the chapter, making notes in your book and underlining or highlighting sections that interest you.

This practice will prepare you to better answer the questions found in the study guide. Since Lewis tends to be a very verbose writer, I have provided definitions and descriptions to various references that you will find at the end of each session in the study guide as well as a full summary of each chapter in the back of the study guide. You will also find the page numbers next to each question to better help you locate the answer.

In addition, you will find the answers to each question in the study guide online at www.BrownChairBooks.com. However, do not cheat yourself. Work through each session prior to viewing the answers. A downloadable Scripture Reference Guide is also available online to save time spent looking up Scripture in class.

## GROUP FORMAT

For group formats, the study works best over an eleven-week period. The first week is an introduction week to hand out study guides (if purchased by the church), read through the introduction, and set a plan and schedule for the remaining ten weeks. You might also have those who have previously read the book share their thoughts and experiences.

This study can certainly be used by Sunday school classes, but recognize that Sunday morning time in many churches is relatively short. Thus, the study lends itself very well to midweek times at the church or in the homes of members.

Session length is variable. Ideally, you should allow at least 90 minutes per session. For longer sessions, take a quick refreshment break in the middle.

If you're the group leader, your role will be to facilitate the group sessions using the study guide and the answers found at www.BrownChairBooks.com. Recognize that you are the facilitator. You are not the answer person, you are not the authority, and you are not the judge to decide if responses are right or wrong. You are simply the person who tries to keep the discussion on track and in the timeframe allowed while keeping everyone involved, heard, and respected.

## LEARNING ENVIRONMENT

The following are some suggestions for shaping the learning environment for group sessions that help manage time, participation, and confidentiality.

- Ask the Holy Spirit for help as you prepare for the study. Pray for discernment for each member of the group, including yourself.
- Before each session, familiarize yourself with the questions and answers as it may have been several days since you completed the session. Consider reading the weekly chapters again.
- Be prepared to adjust the session as group members interact and questions arise. Allow for the Holy Spirit to move in and through the material, the group members, and yourself.
- Arrange the meeting space to enhance the learning process. Group members should be seated around a table or in a circle so that they can all see one another. Moveable chairs are best.

- Download the quick Bible reference handout at www.BrownChairBooks.com, and distribute it at the beginning of class to save time looking up Scripture.

- If using Bibles, bring extras for those who forget to bring one or for those who might not have one. (If someone is reading aloud, you might ask the person to identify from which Bible translation he or she is reading.)

- If your teaching style includes recording responses from participants or writing questions or quotations for discussion on a board, you may want access to a whiteboard or an easel.

- Agree on the class schedule and times. In order to maintain continuity, it would be best if your class meets for eleven consecutive weeks.

- The suggested session time is 90 minutes. Because each chapter can lead to substantial discussion, you may need to make choices about what you will cover, or you may choose to extend your group sessions to allow more time for discussion.

- Create a climate where it is safe to share. Encourage group members to participate as they feel comfortable. Remember that some will be eager to give answers or offer commentary, while others will need time to process and think.

- If you notice that some participants are hesitant to enter the conversation, ask if they have thoughts to share. Give everyone an opportunity to talk, but keep the conversation moving. Intervene when necessary to prevent a few individuals from dominating the discussion.

- If no one answers at first during a discussion, do not be afraid of silence. Count silently to ten, and then say, "Would anyone like to go first?" If no one responds, provide your own answer and ask for reactions. If you limit your sharing to a surface level, others will follow suit. Keep in mind that if your group is new, cohesion might take a couple of weeks to form. If group members do not share at first, give them time.

- Encourage multiple answers or responses before moving on.

- Ask "Why?" or "Why do you believe that?" or "Can you say more about that?" to draw out greater depth from a response.

- Affirm other's responses with comments such as "Great" or "Thanks" or "Good insight"—especially if this is the first time someone has spoken during the group session.

- Monitor your own contributions. If you are doing most of the talking, back off so that you do not train the group to listen rather than speak.

- Honor the designated time window. Begin on time. If a session runs longer than expected, get consensus from the group before continuing.
- Involve participants in various aspects of the session, such as offering prayer and reading Scripture.
- Because some questions call for sharing personal experiences, confidentiality is essential. Remind group members at each session of the importance of confidentiality and of not passing along stories that have been shared in the group.

## SUGGESTED SESSION OUTLINE

Based on the amount of reading each week, we suggest that you follow the study outline below over an eleven-week period, but you are by no means locked in to this format. The key is group interest and involvement, not the calendar.

| Date | Time | Session | Chapters |
|------|------|---------|----------|
|  |  | Week 1 | Introduction |
|  |  | Week 2 | Preface and Chapter 1 |
|  |  | Week 3 | Chapter 2 |
|  |  | Week 4 | Chapter 3 |
|  |  | Week 5 | Chapter 4 |
|  |  | Week 6 | Chapter 5 |
|  |  | Week 7 | Chapter 6 |
|  |  | Week 8 | Chapter 7 |
|  |  | Week 9 | Chapter 8 |
|  |  | Week 10 | Chapter 9 |
|  |  | Week 11 | Chapter 10 |

# PREFACE

In writing *The Problem of Pain*, C.S. Lewis makes it very clear that much of what he claims in the book is not original but rather "restating ancient and orthodox doctrines," most of which are professed by all believers.

Without a doubt, Lewis is a great writer and a brilliant thinker. His books are filled with incredible insight woven through the depths of a very well-thought-out theology and philosophy. But sometimes he might write something that does not line up with your theology or seems a bit farfetched. Lewis, however, makes it very clear that he is not a Christian theologian but rather "a layman of the Church of England." Therefore, he leaves it up to you to question if you will…which I found myself doing on several occasions.

> *…when pain is to be borne, a little courage helps more than much knowledge, a little human sympathy more than much courage, and the least tincture of the love of God more than all.*

## Discussion Questions

1. Why did C.S. Lewis want to first write *The Problem of Pain* anonymously?

2. What was Lewis's only purpose for writing the book? What did he not intend this book for?

3. The definition of a problem is "any question or matter involving doubt, uncertainty, or difficulty." Although Lewis's quest for the intellectual answer to the problem caused by pain might seem insensitive, why might it be important to first seek to understand the "why" of a problem before we can start proposing a solution?

4. If Lewis was to give any suggestion for bearing pain, what would it be? Do you agree with Lewis? Why or why not?

Answer Guide and Scripture References Available at
**www.BrownChairBooks.com**

Ashley Sampson (1900–1947) was the owner of Centenary Press who invited C.S. Lewis to write *The Problem of Pain* after reading the "smuggled-in theology" in *Out of the Silent Planet*. Geoffrey Bless Ltd., another publisher of Lewis, later bought Centenary Press.

Walter Hilton was an English Augustinian mystic whose works became influential in the 15th century. (Wikipedia)

# CHAPTER 1
# INTRODUCTORY

Lewis starts this introductory chapter on a personal note: "Not many years ago when I was an atheist…" As an atheist, Lewis's objection to God was based on his observed futility of the universe, which included the mass proliferation of pain, suffering, and death of the human race.

He soon finds one problem in his observation: If the universe is as bad as he observes it to be, how could man have ever conceived of an all-loving God in the first place? No human being, destined to undergo pain and suffering and to be erased from all eternity, would ever think to connect it to an all-loving and caring God. Such a conception doesn't simply emerge out of the minds of men.

In the preface, Lewis's stated goal for the book is to "solve the intellectual problem raised by suffering." However, in order to do so, he must first examine the origin of religion and how it creates the problem of pain to begin with.

> *…for pain would be no problem unless, side by side with our daily experience of this painful world, we had received what we think a good assurance that ultimate reality is righteous and loving.*

## Discussion Questions

1. As a former atheist, how would Lewis have responded to anyone asking him why he did not believe in God? What had Lewis concluded about who or what created the universe? Given your own life experiences, have there been times when you struggled with the same question? Explain. (pp. 1–3)

2. At the beginning of this chapter, Lewis uses a short quotation from Pascal, who criticizes the attempts of others to prove the existence of God from the works of nature. Pascal goes as far as to say that no "canonical writers" ever used nature to make a case for the existence of God. This, however, is incorrect. Read Psalm 29:3–6, Romans 1:20, Acts 14:15–17, and Job 12:7–9. According to Scripture, what does nature reveal, if anything, about God?

3. Regarding the universe, what was the one question that Lewis never dreamed of raising as an atheist? (p. 3)

4. Some might say that religion was developed in the fearful minds of our ignorant ancestors, who created the idea of a wise and good God. What does Lewis say is wrong with this assumption? (pp. 4–5)

5. Lewis proposes that religion from its very beginning has included three elements (with Christianity proposing one more). The first element is the Numinous. Describe the Numinous. Why is the feeling of awe and dread of the supernatural (the Numinous) innate in all humans? (pp. 5–7)

6. Using current and historical literature, Lewis states that we do not know how far back in human history the feeling of the supernatural goes. It somehow came into existence, is widespread, and "does not disappear from the mind with the growth of knowledge and civilization." How does our world today attempt to explain the supernatural? What sources seek to influence our understanding of the supernatural? (pp. 7–8)

7. Describe the second element found in all religions, the "moral experience." What is the one commonality found in all moralities throughout time? (pp. 10–11)

8. Describe the third element found in all religions. Why is it not obvious why man would link the first two elements found in all religions? (pp. 11–12)

9. Describe the historical incarnation, or the fourth element that is unique to Christianity. (p. 13)

10. Read John 10:30, John 8:58, Luke 22:70, Matthew 28:18, John 5:17–22, John 14:6, John 11:25, and Mark 14:61–62. Who does Jesus say that He is? What are the only two possible views of Jesus Christ?

11. How might becoming a Christian change your perception of God from awe and dread to hope? (pp. 13–14)

12. How does not believing in Jesus Christ (the historical incarnation) impact your opinion of God?

13. What are the consequences of rebelling against the supernatural or disregarding morality? What are the consequences of ignoring the Numinous with morality? (pp. 14–15)

14. How does Christianity create rather than solve the problem of pain? Do you struggle with identifying the reason for pain? What are some conclusions you've arrived at? (pp. 14–15)

## CHAPTER 1 NOTES AND REFERENCES

Answer Guide and Scripture References Available at
**www.BrownChairBooks.com**

Blaise Pascal was a French mathematician, physicist, inventor, writer, and Catholic theologian. He was a child prodigy who was educated by his father, a tax collector, in Rouen. When he was about thirty-five, Pascal began to prepare *An Apology [Defense] for the Christian Religion*. He died at thirty-nine, however, before it was completed—leaving only a collection of notes. These were published after his death under the title, *Pensees* ("Thoughts"). – Wikipedia

Claudius Ptolemy was a Greco-Roman mathematician, astronomer, geographer, astrologer, and poet of a single epigram in *The Greek Anthology*. – Wikipedia

Theodicy: The defense of faith and God's goodness in light of suffering and the existence of evil

Rudolf Otto was an eminent German Lutheran theologian, philosopher, and comparative religionist. He is regarded as one of the most influential scholars of religion in the early twentieth century and is best known for his concept of the numinous, a profound emotional experience he argued was at the heart of the world's religions. – Wikipedia

Numinous: A term coined by German theologian Rudolf Otto to describe a sense of the mysterious, supernatural, and holy that incorporates both awe and dread.

*The Wind in the Willows* is a children's novel by Kenneth Grahame, first published in 1908. Alternately slow moving and fast-paced, it focuses on four anthropomorphized animals in a pastoral version of Edwardian England. – Wikipedia

William Wordsworth was a major English Romantic poet who, with Samuel Taylor Coleridge, helped to launch the Romantic Age in English literature with their joint publication, *Lyrical Ballads*. – Wikipedia

Sir Thomas Malory (flourished c. 1470), English writer whose identity remains uncertain but whose name is famous as that of the author of *Le Morte d'Arthur*, the first prose account in English of the rise and fall of the legendary King Arthur and the fellowship of the Round Table. – britannica.com

Publius Ovidius Naso, known as Ovid in the English-speaking world, was a Roman poet who lived during the reign of Augustus. – Wikipedia

Publius Vergilius Maro, usually called Virgil or Vergil in English, was an ancient Roman poet of the Augustan period. He wrote three of the most famous poems in Latin literature: the *Eclogues*, the *Georgics*, and the epic *Aeneid*. – Wikipedia

Aeschylus was an ancient Greek tragedian. He is often described as the father of tragedy. Academics' knowledge of the genre begins with his work, and understanding of earlier tragedies is largely based on inferences from his surviving plays. – Wikipedia

Chloroform – A colorless, volatile, sweet-smelling liquid used as a solvent and formerly as a general anesthetic. To render (someone) unconscious with chloroform.

A priori – Relating to or denoting reasoning or knowledge that proceeds from theoretical deduction rather than from observation or experience.

Anfractuosity – A winding channel or course; especially: an intricate path or process (as of the mind)

# CHAPTER 2
# DIVINE OMNIPOTENCE

Is God powerless in the face of suffering?

As Christians, we believe that God is omnipotent, or all powerful over all things at all times and in all ways. But every day we are bombarded with reports of neglect, murders, wars, and natural disasters that seem so unnecessary. If He exists and has the power to make things better, why doesn't He act to remove evil and pain from the face of the earth?

This is a troubling question that drives many people away from God—not necessarily because the question is hard to understand but because the answer is not what we want it to be. In this chapter, Lewis tackles this question head on by helping us understand the balance between God's omnipotence and the self-imposed limitations that He places on Himself for our benefit.

> *If God were good, He would wish to make His creatures perfectly happy, and if God were almighty, He would be able to do what He wished. But the creatures are not happy. Therefore God lacks either goodness, or power, or both.*

## Discussion Questions

1. Lewis simplifies the problem of pain down to "If God were good, then we'd be happy, and if God were almighty, His creatures would also be happy." What does Lewis say is the only possibility of answering the problem of pain? What are the popular meanings today for the words "happy," "good," and "almighty," and how might they fall short when referencing God? (p. 16)

2. The Bible says that God is omnipotent (all-powerful) and "nothing is impossible" for Him. Read Genesis 1:3, 6, 9; Jeremiah 32:17; Luke 1:37; Matthew 19:26; Psalm 135:6; and Job 42:2. What sense of God's power, or omnipotence, do you get from these verses?

3. Lewis states that God's omnipotence is constrained by three realities. The first reality is that even though God is all-powerful, He cannot contradict Himself by doing what is intrinsically impossible *(or contrary to His nature)*. According to 2 Timothy 2:13, James 1:13, Job 34:12, and Hebrews 6:18, what are some of the things that God will not do because it is contrary to His nature?

4. According to Lewis, it's not that God can't do anything but rather that He refuses to act outside of His nature. In the same way, we self-impose limits on ourselves that are motivated by the very nature of who we are. What is an example of something that you could do but refuse to do because it goes against your nature?

5. What are the traits of someone who is constantly contradicting themselves? Do you trust them? Why or why not? What would be the result of having a God who is constantly contracting Himself?

6. The world would have us believe that the Bible is full of contradictions. Read Genesis 3:1–5. From the beginning, how did Satan seek to contradict the authority of God's Word with Eve in the Garden of Eden? How does he continue to cast subtle attacks on believers today?

7. The second reality of God's restrained omnipotence is His greatest gift at creation to our first human parents, Adam and Eve: the gift of free will. Read Deuteronomy 30:15–19 and Joshua 24:15. Why did God give us free will? What would happen if God intervened every time we abused our free will and were about to choose badly?

8. Since we have the freedom to choose, who is ultimately responsible for the consequences of the choices we make? Read Matthew 22:35–40. What does God ultimately desire for us to do with our freedom of choice?

9. The third reality of God's restrained omnipotence is that He created a relatively independent and fixed environment (space and time) for the free beings to live in. Why is it necessary for this environment to have a fixed nature? (pp. 21–22)

10. The earth was not originally created to produce devastating natural disasters. Read Genesis 3:17–19. What effect did sin have on the earth? According to Romans 8:19–21, what is creation eagerly awaiting?

11. It is unfortunate that God gets the blame for senseless acts of violence and that natural disasters are referred to as "acts of God." Yet God is given no credit for months, years, and even decades of peace and good weather. Why do you think this is so? Why doesn't God just intervene in the form of miracles all the time to rescue us? (p. 25)

12. Do you agree with Lewis's statement: "Try to exclude the possibility of suffering…and you find that you have excluded life itself"? Why or why not? (p. 25)

Answer Guide and Scripture References Available at
**www.BrownChairBooks.com**

Saint Thomas Aquinas (1225 – March 7, 1274) was an Italian Dominican friar, Catholic priest, and Doctor of the Church. He was an immensely influential philosopher, theologian, and jurist in the tradition of scholasticism, within which he is also known as the Doctor Angelicus and the Doctor Communis. – Wikipedia

Equivocal – Open to more than one interpretation; uncertain or questionable in nature

Intrinsically – Something associated with a person or thing's nature or inherent characteristics and doesn't depend on external factors; in an essential or natural way

Self-contradictory – To say or do the opposite of something. For example, a teenager might say that he was at the library studying at 8 p.m. for four hours but then later say that he was at the movies the same night.

Inadvertence – The act of not focusing the mind on a matter

Inexorable – Impossible to stop or prevent

Platonic – (of love or friendship) intimate and affectionate but not sexual

Surreptitiously – In a way that attempts to avoid notice or attention; secretively

Externality – The fact of existing outside the perceiving subject

Omniscience – Knowing everything

Plurality – Relating to, consisting of, or containing more than one or more than one kind or class; a plural society

Anthropomorphic – Described or thought of as having a human form or human attributes

Indeterminacy – The indeterminacy of something is its quality of being uncertain or vague

# CHAPTER 3
# DIVINE GOODNESS

Was it "good" for God to make a world that was destined to lead to human suffering? It all depends on your definition of what "good" is.

In this chapter, Lewis takes a look at our understanding of what it means for God to be good. As believers, we believe in an all-loving God who is completely and divinely good. But what is divine goodness, and how is it different from human goodness?

Lewis insists that although there might be some similarities, God's goodness is vastly different from ours. It is better, higher, and greater and includes such things as discipline and suffering—traits that we might not associate with human goodness. But God's goodness is also different from human goodness in that its purpose is always for our benefit.

> *You asked for a loving God; you have one. Not a senile benevolence,*
> *but a consuming, purifying fire.*

## Discussion Questions

1. Lewis says that as we consider God's goodness, we are immediately faced with two dilemmas. What is the first dilemma? Read Romans 8:28. If God's goodness differs from ours, how might this verse help you cope with difficult life situations? (p. 28)

2. What is the second dilemma when considering God's goodness? In Mark 10:17–22, where does Jesus say goodness flows from? Why did the young ruler go away sad? How do you respond to someone who believes they will be in heaven because they have lived a good life? (pp. 28–29)

3. These two dilemmas naturally lead us to question how we are to know what is good if God's standard of goodness is so different than ours. Lewis said the only "escape from this dilemma" of God's goodness is found by observing natural human relations. Describe Lewis's point illustrated through his own experience. (pp. 29–30)

4. Lewis argues that even though our conception of good and evil is different from God's, the differences are a matter of degree, not substance. Using the illustration of a child learning to draw, how does our understanding of God's view of goodness change as we mature in our faith? (p. 30)

5. Do you think, as Lewis suggests, that what people really want is a benevolent grandfather in heaven who does not care what we do as long as we are happy and satisfied? Why or why not? How does our culture reinforce this concept? (p. 31)

6. Compare and contrast love and kindness according to Lewis. (pp. 32–33)

7. Lewis uses four analogies to explain God's love for humanity. The first analogy that he illustrates is the way an artist feels about his artifact. Read Jeremiah 18:1–6 and 1 Peter 2:5. How does understanding that you are a "divine work of art" change how you view God and the role He plays in your life? What is the one limitation to this analogy? (pp. 34–35)

8. The second analogy, and perhaps a better one, is to understand God's love for man is like that of the love of a man for a beast. Why is this a better analogy than the previous one? What is the limitation with this analogy? (pp. 35–36)

9. When we wish that God would just leave us alone to our own impulses, what are really asking of Him? (p. 35)

10. The third analogy of God's love for man is that of a father's love for his son. Lewis suggests that fatherhood in the days of Jesus was regarded much more importantly than fatherhood today. Look at the following statistics below regarding fatherhood in the United States. According to these statistics, why might some people have difficulty associating a loving father with God?

- An estimated 24.7 million children (33%) live absent their biological father. Millions more have dads who are physically present but emotionally absent. *Source: U.S. Census Bureau, Current Population Survey. 2010*

- Of students in grades 1 through 12, thirty-nine percent (17.7 million) live in homes absent their biological fathers. *Source: Nord, Christine Winquist, and Jerry West. Fathers' and Mothers' Involvement in their Children's Schools by Family Type and Resident Status. 2001.*

- A total of 57.6% of black children, 31.2% of Hispanic children, and 20.7% of white children are living absent their biological fathers. *Source: Family Structure and Children's Living Arrangements 2012.*

- According to 72.2 % of the U.S. population, fatherlessness is the most significant family or social problem facing America. *Source: National Center for Fathering, Fathering in America Poll, January 1999.*

11. The fourth and final analogy of God's love for man is that of a man's love for a woman. Lewis makes this illustration through the following verses: Jeremiah 2:2, Ezekiel 16:6–15, James 4:4–5, and Ephesians 5:25–27. Compare God's love for His church and a man's love for his bride. (pp. 38–39)

12. Lewis said that the problem with reconciling human suffering with the existence of a loving God is unsolvable as long as we attach a trivial meaning to the word _____ and if we believe that we are _____. (p. 40)

13. God is in the process of refining us, which can be a painful process. The question is whether we trust Him in this endeavor. How do you feel about God refining you? Do you appreciate friends who confront you and hold you accountable for your behavior even if it jeopardizes your happiness, or would you rather have a friend who lets things go? (p. 42)

14. If we were to attribute the various types of love described in this chapter to humans, it would be described as selfish and possessive because of our needy human nature. How does Lewis address the suggestion that God's love for humans is selfish and possessive? (pp. 43–44)

15. Read Acts 17:25. Does God need our love and praise? If God doesn't need anything, then why does He command us to serve, worship, and give our money to Him?

16. In the end, Lewis says that there are only three alternatives in this world in regards to goodness. What are they?

---

Answer Guide and Scripture References Available at
**www.BrownChairBooks.com**

---

Thomas Traherne was an English poet, clergyman, theologian, and religious writer. Little is known about his life. (1636–1674) – Wikipedia

The doctrine of total depravity is an acknowledgement that the Bible teaches that as a result of the Fall of man (Genesis 3:6), every part of man—his mind, will, emotions, and flesh—have been corrupted by sin. In other words, sin affects all areas of our being, including who we are and what we do. – Got Questions.org

Coterminous – Having the same boundaries or extent in space, time, or meaning

Sentient – Able to perceive or feel things

Intolerable compliment – A polite expression of praise or admiration that is able to be endured

Anthropomorphic – Having human characteristics

Waif – A homeless and helpless person, especially a neglected or abandoned child

Impassible – Incapable of experiencing emotion or pain; theologians have debated whether this is an attribute of God.

Ephraim – The second of Joseph's sons; when used in the Old Testament prophetic books, it refers to the last piece of the northern kingdom of Israel to be carried into Assyrian captivity.

Insoluble – Impossible to solve

King Cophetua – A painting by Sir Edward Burne-Jones as well as a poem by Tennyson, based on the legend of an African king who had no interest in women until he saw a beggar maid, fell instantly in love with her, and made her his queen

Egoistic – Excessive concern for oneself with or without exaggerated feelings of self-importance

Altruistic – Unselfishly concerned for or devoted to the welfare of others

Viola – Viola is the heroine and protagonist of the play *Twelfth Night*, written by William Shakespeare.

Solecism – A grammatical mistake in speech or writing

Erscheinung – Appearance

Despot – A ruler or other person that holds absolute power, typically one who exercises it in a cruel or oppressive way

Milton – John Milton wrote the epic poem, *Paradise Lost*.

George McDonald – George MacDonald was a Scottish author, poet, and Christian minister.

# CHAPTER 4
# HUMAN WICKEDNESS

If there's a God and He's all powerful and all loving, why does He want me to change? What have I done to Him that's so bad that I need to change? I don't think I'm that bad. In fact, when I look around at others in society, I seem rather good compared to some of them.

The simple and easy Christian answer is that none of us are good in the sense that God requires. We're all sinners, every one of us. God wants to make us more lovable by making us more like Jesus Christ.

Unfortunately, the problem in today's culture is that we do not think we need God. The shame of sin and bad behavior has diminished over time and, in some respects, has become fashionable and even accepted as normal behavior.

Cultural alleviation of the shame of sin will never override the pain, suffering, and consequences that sin actually produces. In this chapter, Lewis helps us understand the nature of human wickedness and what needs to be altered to make us better.

> *We think the worst we have done to God is to leave him alone.*
> *Why can't he return the compliment?*

## Discussion Questions

1. Lewis claims the gospel was first preached to those who were more aware of their shame, even those from pagan backgrounds as "they knew they deserved the Divine anger." He believes the philosophies of the modern age have lured people into a false hope of believing their sin and shame no longer require a God-sized solution. Lewis attributes this to two principal causes. What is the first principal cause? What is the second principal cause? (pp. 49–50)

2. Regardless of cultural reinterpretation of sin, Scripture is very clear on the subject matter. According to Isaiah 59:2 and Romans 6:23, what is the consequence of sin in regard to our relationship with God? Many would like to believe that God is so "loving" that He will overlook our "little faults," "lapses," and "indiscretions." Read Jeremiah 16:17, Numbers 32:23, and Hebrews 4:13. Why is it wrong for us to think that God will overlook our sin, even small, relatively unimportant things?

3. Lewis says regarding the view of sin in society that "We are told to 'get things out into the open', not for the sake of self-humiliation, but on the grounds that these 'things' are very natural and we need not be ashamed of them." What sins today are excused as natural expressions of who we are? (p. 50)

4. Read Ephesians 4:18–19 and 1 Corinthians 2:14. How does Paul describe a culture that has chosen to indulge in sin? According to Romans 1:24–28 what are the consequences for a culture when sin goes unaddressed in society?

5. What does Lewis say is the only solution to saving a culture that has co-opted this mindset regarding sin? According to Lewis, what happens when people attempt to be Christians without an awareness of sin? According to 1 John 1:8–10 what happens when we attempt to be Christians without an awareness of sin? (pp. 50–51)

6. Lewis makes eight observations as to why the modern-day illusion of innocence is just that—an illusion. What is the first modern-day illusion of innocence? Why is this particular illusion so tempting and easy for us? What did Paul say is the danger of making comparisons with one another in 2 Corinthians 10:12? (pp. 52–53)

7. What is the second modern-day illusion of innocence? What is the danger of succumbing to the idea of "corporate guilt?" (p. 54)

8. What is the third modern-day illusion of innocence? Read 2 Peter 3:8. Why should we not evaluate our sin by the time that has lapsed? (pp. 54–55)

9. What is the fourth modern-day illusion of innocence? Have you ever used this excuse? When we use this excuse, we are attempting to shift the standards of righteousness to meet our personal or social agendas. According to Isaiah 5:20, why should we not attempt this shift in morality? What are some examples of society shifting the standards of morality? (pp. 55–57)

10. What is the fifth modern-day illusion of innocence? Do you think the level of morality in society today is better than that of our ancestors? (p. 58)

11. What is the sixth modern-day illusion of innocence? What is an example that Lewis used of a virtue being used outside of God's moral law? (p. 59)

12. What is the seventh modern-day illusion of innocence? (pp. 59–60)

13. What is the eighth modern-day illusion of innocence? What did James say about where temptation comes from in James 1:13–15? Do you think that some people are born genetically geared toward certain behaviors? Explain. How does this fit in with shifting responsibility of that behavior back to God? (p. 60)

14. Review the definition of the Doctrine of Total Depravity in the notes section. What was Lewis's position on total depravity? Do you agree with him?

15. In this chapter, Lewis desires for us to understand intellectually (not emotionally) that we are in some respects a "horror to God" and that the closer we get to God, the more we realize it. How does the apostle Paul characterize himself in 1 Timothy 1:15?

---

Answer Guide and Scripture References Available at
**www.BrownChairBooks.com**

---

Epicurean philosophy – A philosophy of one devoted to sensual pleasure

Psychoanalysis – A system of psychological theory and therapy that aims to treat mental disorders by investigating the interaction of conscious and unconscious elements in the mind and bringing repressed fears and conflicts into the conscious mind by techniques such as dream interpretation and free association

Nadir – The lowest point; the point of greatest adversity or despair

Extirpate – To root out and destroy completely.

Pons asinorum (Latin for "bridge of asses") is the name given to Euclid's fifth proposition in his Elements of geometry, also known as the theorem on isosceles triangles…the first real test in the Elements of the intelligence of the reader and functions as a "bridge" to the harder propositions that follow. Whatever its origin, the term is also used as a metaphor for a problem or challenge which will separate the sure of mind from the simple, the fleet thinker from the slow, the determined from the dallier; to represent a critical test of ability or understanding. – Wikipedia

Iniquitous – Grossly unfair and morally wrong

Quixotic – Exceedingly idealistic; unrealistic and impractical

William Law (1686 – April 9, 1761) was an English priest, writer, and mystic. – Wikipedia

Doctrine of Total Depravity – While often misunderstood, the doctrine of total depravity is an acknowledgement that the Bible teaches that as a result of the Fall of man (Genesis 3:6), every part of man—his mind, will, emotions, and flesh—has been corrupted by sin. In other words, sin affects all areas of our being, including who we are and what we do. It acknowledges that the Bible teaches that we sin because we are sinners by nature. – GotQuestions.org

# CHAPTER 5
# THE FALL OF MAN

If we are wicked at our core, then how could we have ever come from the hands of a good and loving God? The Christian response is to say that our wicked nature did not come from the hands of a good and loving God but rather we were initially good and then abused our freedom and made ourselves the wicked creatures we are now.

But what was the origin of events that led to humanity becoming vile and a horror to God, and how does this reinforce the notion that suffering is a natural response to sin?

What follows in this chapter is Lewis's creative evolutionary description of the Fall of man. Depending on your background, some of Lewis's statements in this chapter may be unsettling and even disturbing as he attempts to merge evolution with the biblical story of creation in Genesis. At other times, he refers to biblical stories as "myths in Holy Scripture" and states that "for long centuries God perfected the animal form" when referring to the creation of man.

In so much as you may disagree with some of Lewis's statements in this chapter, the key to take away is not Lewis's interpretation of the events surrounding the Fall but that the Fall of man is what led to sin entering the world.

> *What Man lost by the Fall was his original specific nature.*

## Discussion Questions

1. According to Lewis, what is the Christian answer to the doctrine of the Fall? A religion that believes there's only one god might struggle with explaining the origins of evil. For example, one might say, "Did God create evil?" or "Why does He permit it?" What two theories on the origin of evil does Lewis say the doctrine of the Fall guards against? (p. 63)

2. The theories of monism and dualism are not taught anywhere in Scripture. In contrast, monotheism is the belief in a one true God who is the only creator, sustainer, and judge of all creation and who created all things good. How do the following verses support the idea of a monotheistic God? Genesis 1:1, Deuteronomy 4:35, Deuteronomy 6:4, Malachi 2:10a, 1 Corinthians 8:6, and James 2:19

3. What two functions does Lewis say the doctrine of the Fall does not address? How does Paul explain the consequences of Adam's sin for him and us in Romans 5:12–14, 18–19? (p. 64)

4. Do you think God should have simply erased the results of the first sin and given humanity a second chance? How does Lewis work through this proposition? (p. 65)

5. Regarding science, some say that the Fall is disproved by modern science, meaning that the human race has made advancement and refinement and has slowly risen out of brutality and savagery. What was Lewis's interesting response to that claim? Do you agree with Lewis or disagree? Explain your answer. (pp. 66–67)

6. Regarding philosophy, some say Adam could not have committed the first sin because there were no laws to sin against since laws had not been developed yet. How does Lewis respond to this philosophy? Reread Romans 5:12–13. What does this passage make clear about when sin entered the world in regard to the law? (p. 69)

7. St. Augustine calls the first sin the result of pride. From the moment a creature becomes aware of God as God and itself as self, it has the terrible alternative of choosing itself over God. No matter who we are, we all struggle with choosing self over God in everyday matters. How did Paul characterize his struggle with sin in Romans 7:19? Do you also sometimes feel this way about your sin? (pp. 69–70)

8. Lewis takes some creative liberties with his interpretation of the creation story. Summarize Lewis's account of what happened when man fell? (pp. 72–75)

9. The act of self-will is the only sin that can be conceived of at the Fall. Daily, we must make an act of self-surrender, however small or easy, in living to our God-given purposes rather than ourselves. Read Psalm 37:7, Matthew 16:24–25, Proverbs 3:5–6, and Romans 12:1. According to these verses, what are some steps we can take in surrendering our self-will to God each day? (p. 76)

10. Genesis 2:7 says that the human spirit is the very breath of God that was breathed into man at creation. Before the Fall, the human spirit obeyed and loved God without painful effort and had full control over its consciousness, intellect, emotions, fears, passions, and creativity, not to mention possessing a free will—a gift that no other creature had. Describe the condition of the human spirit after the Fall. (p. 77)

11. According to 1 Corinthians 2:11–16, what frame of reference does the natural man use to try to understand spiritual things? In what way does this hinder him? What frame of reference does the spiritual man use to try to understand all things? Does the "natural" man understand the actions of the "spiritual" man? Why or why not? List some specific examples of things he cannot comprehend.

12. Lewis said that once the human spirit began to revolt, God began to rule the creature not by the laws of the spirit but by those of nature. The organs, no longer governed by man's will, fell under the control of ordinary biochemical laws and suffered whatever the inner-workings of those laws might bring about in the way of pain, senility, and death. The will, caught in the tidal wave of mere nature, had no resource but to force back some of the new thoughts and desires, and these became the subconscious as we now know it (pp. 77–78). Consider the following proper laws, and describe what their natural law consequence might be:

Gluttony:

Alcohol abuse:

Drugs:

Sexually promiscuity:

Gossip and badmouthing others:


13. Lewis contends that the Fall did not take God by surprise nor did God plan the whole thing. Instead, Lewis describes the world as a dance. What "steps" make up that dance? (p. 80)



14. Read 1 Corinthians 15:21–22. Lewis seems to struggle with Paul's statement that we "die in Adam and live in Christ." What do you believe Paul is saying in this passage?

---

Answer Guide and Scripture References Available at
**www.BrownChairBooks.com**

---

Monism and Dualism – In simple terms, monism is the belief that ultimately the mind and the brain are the same thing, whereas dualists believe that the mind and the brain are separate.

Profundity – Deep insight; great depth of knowledge or thought

The Socratic method is a style of education involving a conversation in which a student is asked to question their assumptions. It is a forum for open-ended inquiry, one in which both student and teacher can use probing questions to develop a deeper understanding of the topic.

Original sin – Refers to the sin of Adam and Eve in Genesis 3, the effects of which were passed on to their descendants (Romans 5:12, 19)

Pons asinorum – Latin for "bridge of asses"; refers to the fifth proposition in Book One of Euclid's Elements, which holds that angles opposite the same length sides of an isosceles triangle are equal. Metaphorically, it means a problem that tests the ability of the                                                                                          inexperienced.

Gautama (563–483 BCE) – The spiritual leader on whose teachings Buddhism is based

Zarathustra aka Zoroaster – Persian founder of Zoroastrianism

Marcus Aurelius (121–180) – Stoic philosopher and Roman emperor who wrote *Meditations*

William Law (1686–1761) – Anglican clergyman and devotional writer. In 1729 he wrote *A Serious Call to a Devout and Holy Life*, which argued that Christianity affects every area of life, including business and leisure as well as devotional practices.

N.P. Williams (1883–1943) – Professor of divinity and editor of *Theology*, which represented liberal Catholicism

Meum – Latin for "mine"

Richard Hooker (1554–1600) – Oxford-educated minister in the Church of England. His best-known work is *Of the Laws of Ecclesiastical Polity*, published in eight volumes, the last three posthumously. The series is both a response to Puritan doctrine and a guide for church governance. Considered one of the best examples of Elizabethan literature, the work influenced political theory and English prose as well as theology.

Patristic Doctrine – In the Age of the Church Fathers (patristic from the Latin, pater, for father), leaders in the early Church established doctrines that defined Christian orthodoxy and developed institutions that shaped Christianity for its second millennium.

Anselm's Doctrine – The satisfaction theory of atonement is a theory in Christian theology that Jesus Christ suffered crucifixion as a substitute for human sin, satisfying God's just wrath against humankind's transgression due to Christ's infinite merit. The theory draws primarily from the works of Anselm of Canterbury.

Pantheism – A doctrine that identifies God with the universe or regards the universe as a manifestation of God

# CHAPTER 6
# HUMAN PAIN

What part does pain play in correcting our wicked nature?

In this fallen world, every part of our spiritual nature is inclined to put up barriers between ourselves and God, yet God has a different plan that involves tearing down those barriers and surrendering our will to His. He does so in a way that maintains His goodness while respecting man's freedom—by allowing us to experience pain and suffering.

Pain, by its very nature, hurts, and obviously we would like to avoid it at all costs. But only through pain do we realize that all is not well, that we cannot handle it, and that we need a force bigger than ourselves to find a solution for the pain.

This is not an easy concept to understand as suffering can produce good things within a person while also seeming to cause harm to others. But for the sake of this chapter, consider your pain an opportunity to share in the sufferings of Jesus Christ.

> *God whispers to us in our pleasures, speaks in our conscience,*
> *but shouts in our pains: it is His megaphone to rouse a deaf world.*

**Discussion Questions**

1. Lewis said, "The possibility of pain is inherent in a world where souls can meet." In fact, Lewis credits 80% of pain and suffering to the result of human wickedness. Do you agree or disagree with his estimate? Explain your answer. (p. 86)

2. What are the two senses in which the word "pain" is used, and which one is the focus of this chapter? (pp. 87–88)

3. What is the "proper good" of a creature, and what is the result of that "good"? Why is self-improvement not enough for us to be "properly good"? (p. 88)

4. According to Luke 9:23, Psalm 37:7, and Galatians 2:20, what does it mean to "lay down our arms" and surrender to God? Why is surrendering our will to God so painful? Describe Lewis' analogy of a child surrendering their will to another authority. (pp. 88-89)

5. Lewis writes that surrendering our will is actually made easier by the presence of pain. He identifies three ways in which suffering and pain are useful for our corrective good. The first way is when pain shatters our illusion that all is well with our life. What sort of life events can shatter your illusion that all is well? How can this pain either lead you to or cause you to rebel against God? (pp. 90–93)

6. Lewis says that pain is God's "megaphone to rouse a deaf world." Have you experienced a season of pain that jarred what you perceived to be a good life? According to Paul, what is the proper response to suffering in Romans 5:3–5?

7. Have you ever found yourself thinking regarding someone else's pain that they might actually have deserved it? According to Lewis, why might we sometimes think that way? (p. 91)

8. The second way in which suffering and pain are useful for our corrective good is when our self-sufficient attitude is completely shattered by the weight of pain. What life events might lead you to realize that you simply lack the means (apart from God) to cope with your situation? (pp. 94–96)

9. How does Jesus describe our dependence on Him in John 15:5? What can we do apart from Him?

10. Like a good and loving Father, God is willing to accept us even when we come to Him as a last resort. What would be the outcome if everyone waited to come to God until they had the purest and best motives? (pp. 94–95)

11. Why might a prostitute, a criminal, or an addict find it easier to turn to God than a well-educated, sober, successful individual? (p. 96)

12. The third way in which suffering and pain are useful for our corrective good is when we learn to surrender to God even when it is painful to do so. Before the Fall, it was man's every inclination and pleasure to serve God. After the Fall, we inherited a whole system of desires that ignore God's will. In what life situations might it be painful to follow God? (pp. 97–101)

13. Read Genesis 12:1–12. What is your response to Lewis's question regarding Abraham being called to sacrifice his son Isaac: "If God is omniscient He must have known what Abraham would do, without any experiment; why, then, this needless torture?" Describe the pain and suffering you think Abraham might have felt leading up to the action. (pp. 100–101)

14. Lewis references Hebrews 2:10 when referring to an "old Christian doctrine of being made perfect through suffering." Although this passage is referring to Jesus fully experiencing the sufferings of this world and emerging victorious over them, what application might it also have for us when you apply Hebrews 4:15–16? (p. 105)

15. How does Lewis interpret pain when he is experiencing it rather than writing about it? Why does Lewis say that tribulations in our lives will never cease?

16. Lewis suggests that the world is a "vale of soul-making." In other words, the work of the world is to provide pain and suffering that will hopefully lead us back to God. What does Peter say the purpose of the pain and suffering is in 1 Peter 1:6–7 and 1 Peter 5:10?

Answer Guide and Scripture References Available at
**www.BrownChairBooks.com**

Filial Obedience – The phrase "filial obedience" is generally understood to refer to special duties—specific kinds of actions, services, and attitudes—that children must provide to their parents simply because they are those parents' offspring.

John Henry Newman (1801–1890) – An Anglican priest, poet, and theologian, and later a Catholic cardinal, who was an important and controversial figure in the religious history of England in the 19th century. – Wikipedia

Mortification – Great embarrassment and shame

Masochism – To derive pleasure from inflicting pain on yourself

Sadism – To derive pleasure from inflicting pain on someone else, especially sexual

Thomas Hobbes (1588–1679) was an English philosopher who is considered one of the founders of modern political philosophy. – Wikipedia

Thomas Hardy (1840–1928) – English novelist of the naturalism movement. Raised Anglican, the seeming unfairness and struggles of life caused Hardy to question the Christian view of God. A clergyman asked him how to reconcile the human experience of pain with the goodness of God.

Alfred Edward Housman (1859–1936) – English classicist and poet, best known for a cycle of poems called *A Shropshire Lad*.

Aldous Huxley (1894–1963) – English writer best known for *Brave New World*. Ironically, Lewis, Huxley, and John F. Kennedy all died on the same day, November 22, 1963.

Anatomising – To examine and analyze in detail

Kantianism – a branch of philosophy that follows the works of Immanuel Kant, who believed that rational beings have dignity and should be respected.

William Paley (1743–1805) – A Christian philosopher and apologist best known for his "watchmaker analogy" regarding the existence of God, as set forth in his book, *Natural Theology*. He had some political views that were out of step with his generation, such as the right of the poor to steal if in need of food, a graduated income tax, and a woman's right to pursue a career rather than be dependent upon male relatives. These views are believed to have kept him from advancing in church hierarchy.

C.C.S. – Stands for Casualty Clearing Station, which were small mobile hospitals used during WWI

William Cowper (1731–1800) – English hymn writer and poet. He was a friend of John Newton (who wrote "Amazing Grace") and contributed to the hymnal Newton compiled. Cowper suffered from depression throughout his life and made several suicide attempts. Inkling member Lord David Cecil wrote a biography of Cowper titled *The Stricken Deer* (1929), which is still in print.

# CHAPTER 7
# HUMAN PAIN, CONTINUED

In this chapter, Lewis offers six additional propositions regarding his argument concerning human pain. They are as follows: 1) There are unusual statements concerning suffering within Scripture; 2) suffering is necessary for redemption; 3) painful self-surrender is unique to each person, not political or civil; 4) in this life, God withholds ultimate happiness but gives many lesser joys; 5) no one has ever or will ever experience the sum of human suffering; 6) sin is contagious, while pain is not.

> *If tribulation is a necessary element in redemption, we must anticipate that it will never cease till God sees the world to be either redeemed or no further redeemable.*

## Discussion Questions

1. Lewis offers six additional propositions that must be considered to round out the discussion on human pain. The first one is that there are unusual statements in Scripture about suffering, especially when considering the Beatitudes found in Matthew 5:3 and 5:10. Lewis suggests that if suffering is good, should it not be pursued rather than avoided? How does he answer that question? (p. 110)

2. List the four steps that occur in a fallen and partially redeemed universe in which God makes complex good out of simple evil, and what is the purpose of each? (p. 111)

3. Lewis claims that man will carry out God's purpose no matter how they act. How might a person serve God as a "son or as a tool?" Provide a real-world example of God making complex good out of simple evil. (p.111)

4. Consider the suffering that Joseph experienced at the hands of his brothers in Genesis 37–50. What was Joseph's response to his brothers about their mistreatment of him in Genesis 50:20? (p. 111)

5. Asceticism, what Lewis refers to as self-torture, is the practice of avoiding certain forms of indulgence, typically for religious reasons, like fasting for example. How is this different from pain sent by God? What conclusions does Lewis draw about ascetic practices such as fasting? (pp. 112–113)

6. The second proposition is that since suffering is necessary for redemption, it will not cease until God sees the world as redeemed or as beyond redemption. Why might this statement be discouraging to those seeking to negate suffering by ushering in social and economic reforms?

7. According to Deuteronomy 10:18, 24:17, 27:19; Matthew 25:40; and James 1:27, what should be the Christian view of social justice? How might this be different from the man-centered approach to social justice?

8. Following up on the second proposition, the third proposition is that self-surrender to God is based on personal obedience and is not a model for politics and governments. What role do you believe government should play in caring for the poor and suffering? Why will governmental reforms never fill the role and obligation of the Christian in society? (p. 115)

9. The fourth proposition is that God withholds a settled sense of security and happiness. Why might God withhold "settled happiness"? How should we view the pleasure and joys of this life? (p. 116)

10. How might Hebrews 13:14, 1 Peter 2:11–12, and John 17:14–16 comfort you in times of suffering?

11. The fifth proposition is that human suffering is uniquely personal and not cumulative. In other words, we experience only our own pain and our own suffering and never another's. If you starve to death, you experience all the starvation that ever has been or ever can be. A thousand people starving with you does not increase your pain. What you yourself can suffer is the utmost that can be suffered on Earth. Read Isaiah 53:4. Who is the sole exception to this rule in regard to cumulative suffering? (pp. 116–117)

12. The sixth proposition is that pain is not contagious. When it's over, it's over, and the natural sequel is joy. In this way, how is pain different from sin? (pp. 116–117)

---

Answer Guide and Scripture References Available at
**www.BrownChairBooks.com**

---

Marlowe's lunatic Tamburlaine refers to Christopher Marlowe's 1587 play, *Tamburlaine the Great*.

> Farewell, my boys! My dearest friends, farewell!
> My body feels, my soul doth weep to see
> Your sweet desires depriv'd my company,
> For Tamburlaine, the scourge of God, must die.

Ascetic – characterized by or suggesting the practice of severe self-discipline and abstention from all forms of indulgence, typically for religious reasons

Renunciation – The formal rejection of something, typically a belief

# CHAPTER 8
# HELL

If the ultimate goal of pain is to redeem us and make us more like Christ, what about those who are not redeemed by pain?

The very thought of hell as described by Jesus and the Scriptures conjures up serious objections for those seeking to reconcile how an all-powerful, loving God could assign anyone to this horrible demise.

What Lewis makes clear is that God objects to hell too. In fact, He demonstrates this first by providing a way to Him through the cross and secondly by continuing to pursue us and draw us near to Him—often through pain.

Unfortunately, not everyone will be redeemed, because their love for sin is greater than their love for God. Therefore, hell becomes both moral and a necessity for those who persist in their rebellion.

> *I am not going to try to prove the doctrine tolerable. Let us make no mistake;*
> *it is not tolerable. But I think the doctrine can be shown to be moral...*

**Discussion Questions**

1. Lewis said the doctrine of hell is one of the chief grounds on which Christianity is attacked as barbarous and the grace of God challenged. Lewis, too, detests it, and if he had it in his power, he would willingly remove the doctrine. If you were to poll your friends, family, and acquaintances, what aspect of hell, if any, do you think they would find most difficult to accept?

2. By what four reasons does Lewis claim the doctrine of hell is affirmed? In regard to "reason," why will not all be saved? (pp. 119–120)

3. Christianity is unlike other religions in that it presents a God who assigns hell to some but is also so full of mercy that He becomes man and dies for the sin of all mankind to avert their final ruin if they will just repent. Yet some do, and some don't. According to John 3:19, 1 Corinthians 2:14, and Romans 8:7, what is the reasoning why unrepentant people do not desire God or seek after Him? (p. 121)

4. Lewis agrees that the doctrine of hell is not tolerable but that it is shown to be moral by overcoming five common objections. The first objection is that retribution, or dispensing punishment for bad behavior, is unjust. Summarize Lewis's analogy of a treacherous and cruel man to that of an ethical demand for justice against him. (pp. 121–125)

5. How would you describe the difference between condoning and forgiving? What happens to a culture when sin is condoned instead of forgiven? Why is it easier to condone? (p. 124)

6. We know that a loving God would prefer to see everyone saved, but He also allows humans to control their own destinies and does not force people to be with Him. In *The Great Divorce*, Lewis wrote, "There are only two kinds of people in the end: those who say to God, 'Thy will be done,' and those to whom God says, in the end, 'Thy will be done.'" Do you believe that those who end up in hell actually choose it over heaven? Using the following verses, summarize how man's free will and God's sovereignty work together in salvation.

Romans 8:29 and John 15:16 – Who determines who is saved?

Romans 5:16 – Who takes the first step in salvation?

John 3:16, John 12:32, Romans 10:13, and Titus 2:11 – Who is salvation made available to?

Romans 10:9–10 – What must man do to be saved?

2 Corinthians 5:17 – What is the result of our salvation?

7. The second objection to the doctrine of hell is that eternal punishment doesn't fit the temporal crime. In other words, the annihilation of man to an eternity in hell for sins committed in a short lifespan doesn't seem fair. How does Lewis first handle this objection using the concept of lines and planes? (p. 125)

8. Lewis said there is a similar form of the same objection in that God should give people a second chance after death to respond to Him. How does he respond to this argument? (p. 126)

9. The third objection to the doctrine of hell deals with the frightful intensity of the pains of hell. Lewis categorizes the language of hell used by Christ Himself into three distinct groups: everlasting punishment (Matthew 25:46), destruction (Matthew 10:28), and banishment (Matthew 25:10–13). Why do you think these descriptions are so scary? When you think of family or friends falling into these groups, how does it make you feel? What sort of motivation should these verses have on the redeemed in their efforts to reach the unredeemed? (pp. 126–127)

10. In Matthew 25:34–41, Christ makes it very clear that God has prepared a place for the redeemed and a place for the unredeemed. Describe Lewis's thoughts about what happens to a soul at death? (pp. 127–128)

11. The fourth objection to the doctrine of hell is that the residents of heaven would be sad knowing their loved ones were in hell. Use Revelation 21:4 to counter that objection.

12. The fifth objection to the doctrine of hell is that God isn't omnipotent (all-powerful) if just a single soul rejects God and goes to hell. How does Lewis handle this objection? (pp. 129–130)

13. What do you think Lewis means when he says that the "doors of hell are locked on the *inside*"?

14. On what cautionary note does Lewis conclude the chapter? Do you agree? Explain your answer. (pp. 130–31)

---

*Answer Guide and Scripture References Available at*
**www.BrownChairBooks.com**

---

Dominical – Christians, Christ, the Church

Mahometans – followers of Islam

Thomas Aquinas – Saint Thomas Aquinas OP was an Italian Dominican friar, Catholic priest, and Doctor of the Church. He was an immensely influential philosopher, theologian, and jurist in the tradition of scholasticism, within which he is also known as the Doctor Angelicus and the Doctor Communis. – Wikipedia

Friedrich von Hügel (1852–1925) was an influential Austrian Roman Catholic layman, religious writer, Modernist theologian, and Christian apologist. – Wikipedia

Edwyn Bevan (1870–1943) – A lecturer in Hellenistic history at King's College, London and a historian of comparative religion, Bevan gave the Gifford lectures in 1933 and 1934, which became his books *Symbolism* and *Belief and Holy Images*. He had an interest in India and archeology. During WWI, he worked in British intelligence as well as the Department of Propaganda.

# CHAPTER 9
# ANIMAL PAIN

Why do animals experience suffering and pain, and what, if any relation, does this have to human pain?

The Bible has so little to say about animal pain that this is admittedly in the area of speculation. But for those who are seriously disturbed by the thought of animal pain, Lewis surmises that, lacking consciousness, animals cannot suffer the way humans can suffer. There is no "self" within them to suffer. Animals may have pain but can never experience suffering or reflection upon that pain as a human would.

In this chapter, Lewis speculates on the rationale for animal pain while developing several interesting theories about the possibility of animal immortality.

> *God has given us data which enable us, in some degree, to understand our own suffering: He has given us no such data about beasts. We know neither why they were made nor what they are, and everything we say about them is speculative.*

## Discussion Questions

1. Why can the redemptive aspects of human pain not be extended to animal pain? Why should we not allow animal suffering to become the center of the problem of human pain? (pp. 132–133)

2. Lewis said that "life" in the biological sense has nothing to do with good and evil until the life has the capacity to feel, perceive, or experience subjectively, which animals cannot. What three questions arise when trying to understand animal suffering and pain? (p. 134)

3. In regard to the first question, "What do animals suffer?" what is Lewis's response as to whether or not animals have the same awareness of their suffering as human beings do?

4. What is the difference in the way that humans and animals experience pain? What distinction does Lewis make between sentience (the ability to perceive and experience pain) and consciousness (the state of being aware of one's own existence)? (pp. 134–136)

5. Read Genesis 1:27, 2:7, 2:19, and 7:15. What is the differentiating factor between the creation of animals and human beings? According to 1 Thessalonians 5:23, why is man the only creation of God with the ability to be redeemed through Christ?

6. Admittedly, Lewis was fond of animals. As a child, he abandoned his given name, Clive, and announced that he wanted to be called Jack after his dog, Jacksie, died. The Narnia tales include a variety of animals acting in the best interest of the Christ-like lion, Aslan. Several times in this section, Lewis suggests that some of the higher beasts may have unconscious sentience but that most probably do not. Why is it a natural response for us to want to humanize animals and especially our pets? What did Lewis say that we might have invented because of our fondness for pets? (pp. 136–137)

7. In regard to the second question on animal pain, why does Lewis reject the idea that animal disease, suffering, and death could be traced back to the original sin of human beings? If the origin of animal pain cannot be attributed to human rebellion, what theory does Lewis propose? (p. 137)

8. How does Paul's letter to the church at Rome in Romans 8:18–22 seemingly contradict Lewis's theory of Satan corrupting the animal world prior to the fall of humanity? (p. 137)

9. Supposing Satan did corrupt creation before the creation of man, what redemptive function does Lewis speculate might have been humanity's role had man not fallen? (pp. 137–139)

10. In regard to the third question, whatever the cause of animal suffering, God has permitted it, and since God is good, what will He ultimately do to set things right? Should He provide animals with immortality? Lewis warns that to even ask the question puts one at risk of being dismissed as an "old maid" who is overly preoccupied with her pets. However, he believes animal immortality to be a legitimate question for theological investigation, but where does he admittedly run into difficulty with his theory? (pp. 140–141)

11. Lewis writes, "Man was appointed by God to have dominion over the beasts, and everything man does to an animal is either a lawful exercise, or a sacrilegious abuse, or an authority by Divine right." Read Genesis 1:26–28. What do you think it means for humanity to have dominion over animals? What responsibility comes with that authority?

12. What two reasons might cause Christians to hesitate to believe in animal immortality? (pp. 144–145)

13. Explain Lewis's theory of "derivative immortality" for domesticated animals. Do you agree or disagree with his theory? (p. 145)

14. A better explanation of animal immortality possibly lies within Scripture. Read Romans 8:18–22 and Isaiah 11:6–9. What do these passages suggest?




15. What are your thoughts as to why Lewis included this chapter? Could you have done without it, or was it helpful?

Answer Guide and Scripture References Available at
**www.BrownChairBooks.com**

Sentience – The capacity to feel, perceive or experience subjectively. Eighteenth-century philosophers used the concept to distinguish the ability to think (reason) from the ability to feel.

William Wordsworth was a major English Romantic poet who, with Samuel Taylor Coleridge, helped to launch the Romantic Age in English literature with their joint publication, *Lyrical Ballads.* – Wikipedia

Anaesthetized – Deprived of feeling or awareness

Docetist – Docetism is broadly defined as any teaching that claims that Jesus's body was either absent or illusory.

Hypostatised – Treat or represent (something abstract) as a concrete reality

Systeme de la nature – Representing the laws of the moral and physical worlds

Saturnalia – The ancient Roman festival of Saturn in December, which was a period of general merrymaking and was the predecessor of Christmas

# CHAPTER 10
# HEAVEN

What is the ultimate answer to the problem of pain? Heaven!

In Paul's letter to the Roman church, he tells us that the afflictions, persecutions, sickness, pain, and all that believers are called to endure on this earth last no longer than the present time. These afflictions are but for a moment, for no sooner we are in heaven, where we are free from fears, doubts, disease, death, pains, and wicked people who can hurt us.

In this last chapter, Lewis seeks to balance the scales between the pain we experience here on Earth and the joys of heaven. Heaven is not some illusion that Christians have developed to ease suffering but rather a real place that Christ has prepared for those who believe.

> *Your place in heaven will seem to be made for you and you alone, because you were made for it—made for it stitch by stitch as a glove is made for a hand.*

**Discussion Questions**

1. If you were to poll your family, friends, and acquaintances, how might they describe heaven? Using the following Bible passages, describe the nature of heaven. Does the promise of heaven affect your thinking about pain?

    a)  Matthew 6:20 –

    b)  Luke 23:43 –

    c)  John 14:2 –

    d)  1 Corinthians 2:9 –

    e)  Hebrews 11:16 –

    f)  Revelation 21:4 –

2. Why does Lewis indicate that people might be silent on the subject of heaven, and what is his response to this? Do you find this to be true? Why or why not? (p. 149)

3. Heaven is neither a bribe for goodness nor some "great pie in the sky" reality. Heaven is our desire for love, fellowship, joy, beauty, and union fulfilled for all eternity with the Creator. How does a pure desire for heaven differ from a mercenary desire (one that serves only for what they will get)? How does the thought of heaven comfort you when working through trials and the pains of life? (p. 149)

4. Read 2 Corinthians 5:1–5 and Psalm 84:2. How do these passages support Lewis's claim that within each soul there is a longing for heaven? How does Lewis compare our longing for our favorite books, beautiful landscapes, hobbies, and friendships with the longing for heaven? (pp. 149–150)

5. Why does God make each soul unique? What use does God have for all the differences? (pp. 151–152)

6. Lewis defines the "ultimate law" as abandoning that which we really desire so as to allow it to truly live. How is Matthew 16:25–26 a death blow to self-centered living? What does it mean for us to give our life in order to save it? (p. 154)

7. Lewis believes there will be no ownership in heaven. Using Revelation 2:17, what does he suggest we will receive, and what might that indicate? (p. 154)

8. We most often understand 1 Corinthians 12:12–14 as it is used within the context of the diverse work of believers here on Earth. However, Lewis applies it to the diversity of believers eternally worshipping in heaven. What does Lewis say the result would be if we all experienced and worshipped God identically? (p. 155)

9. God created us distinct from Himself that we might learn to love and "achieve union instead of mere sameness." In other words, God did not create autonomous robots all programmed with the same output but rather individuals with a free will that would continue to become more distinct and reunited with Him. Read Isaiah 43:7 and Romans 8:29–30. How do these verses help a believer define their purpose in life and their relationship to God?

10. Lewis said that a soul's union with God is a continual self-abandonment. We must be "self-giving." Read Galatians 2:20, Luke 9:23, and John 12:24. What does it mean as far as this life is concerned to surrender yourself and be crucified with Christ? Why is God's grace coupled with our faith absolutely necessary for salvation? (pp. 156–157)

11. What is outside the system of self-giving (surrendering yourself to Christ) from which there is no escape? (p. 158)

12. After completing this book and study, what is your understanding about the pain and suffering experienced in life? Is this understanding different from when you started the study? If so, how? Does it also change your understanding about who God is?

Answer Guide and Scripture References Available at
**www.BrownChairBooks.com**

Mercenary soul – One that serves only for what they will get

Brocken spectre – A gigantic shadow of the viewer, which falls on the upper surface of clouds opposite the sun. The phenomenon appears in literature and legends.

Abrogate – To repeal and do away with

# CHAPTER SUMMARIES

## Chapter 1

If I simply look at the world around me and witness the pain, suffering, and regret found in the human race, I have to wonder about the existence of God. In other words, if there is a powerful, wonderful, good, and loving God, why does He allow His creation to suffer? Can He not alleviate our pain even some? If I follow this line of thinking, eventually I will assume that there is no God and that religion is a fantasy made up by our prehistoric, ignorant, and scared ancestors that is now dispelled by science.

But this would be a false assumption because science did not discover pain and suffering. Pain and suffering have been equally felt by all human life throughout time. In fact, man making the connection between world events and a good and wise Creator must have seemed equally ridiculous at all times throughout history. As a result, religion cannot be something that we thought of ourselves or that science can disprove. It has to be separate from us.

If religion is separate from us, what are the forming and common elements? All religions start with a belief in a supernatural power that we hold in reverence and fear. Next, there is a moral standard defining right and wrong behavior. Eventually, we connect the supernatural power with the moral standard. In other words, our God, whom we revere, is also setting the rules for right and wrong. This once again proves that religion is separate from us because man, on his own, would not assign that which he fears to define his morality.

Christianity has one more element than all other religions. Christianity takes the next step with Jesus Christ claiming to be one and the same with the supernatural power as well as the giver of all moral authority. Once we put our faith and trust in Christ, our spiritual eyes are opened to the world around us, and we see things differently.

One of the things we might see differently as a new Christian is that we expect the world to be just, fair, and less painful now, and it is not. This is the problem of pain.

## Chapter 2

If God exists, is good, and has the power to make things better, why doesn't He act to remove evil and pain from the face of the earth and allow us to be perfectly happy creatures?

This question is at the heart of the problem of pain and has created a stumbling block for many who simply cannot get past it. When we consider God, a being who is almighty and who created everything that exists, we don't usually think that there are things God cannot do. However, a deeper study of Scripture helps us understand that it is not because He is unable to act or that His power is limited in any way. Rather, it's because He has restrained His own power for our benefit.

According to Lewis, there are three realities that restrain God's power. First, He will not contradict His own nature. In other words, He will not lie, commit evil, or break His promises. For example, God can never send another flood over the whole earth like He did in Noah's day. It's not that He doesn't possess the ability; He can't do it, because He promised He would never do it again.

Secondly, God provided man with free will. We were created with the freedom to choose. God's plan for our lives is that we would choose Him. Unfortunately, we often do not and find ourselves in sin.

Finally, since God created us with the freedom to choose, then choice implies the existence of things to choose between. For this, He created a world with an "order of nature" for His independent and free beings to live within. This world had to be neutral in the sense that it is not under any person's control. Otherwise, each of us could manipulate it at will. Since nature does not reside under human control, it will be at times favorable to humans and at times not.

Can God suspend the laws of nature and freedom that He has in place and use His power to act within it? Yes, and He does so in the form of miracles, which are evident throughout Scripture and perhaps in our lives. But miracles cannot be commonplace, or they would destabilize the laws of nature and ultimately interfere with our freedom of choice that God desires. In other words, we are not free if our choice is being constantly taken away to prevent harm from being done.

## Chapter 3

The Bible says that God works for the good of those who love Him. But how do we believe such a statement in light of the suffering and pain that we experience that does not seem good? In this chapter, Lewis dives deep into the concept of God's goodness.

The moral dilemma that the question raises about God's goodness provides the perfect excuse for people to abandon a relationship with Jesus Christ. It's hard to reconcile what we perceive to be our good to be evil and what we perceive to be our bad to be our good.

We have to start with the fact that God's goodness is different from human goodness. For example, what we perceive to be good for us, like a close relationship, might actually be bad in the long run. Unfortunately, we cannot see the long run; only God can, so we are left wondering why what we thought was a great relationship failed.

We would prefer to envision God as a fun-loving and doting grandfather who just wants to make his grandkids happy and content. The converse would be a father who genuinely loves and desires to see the best character developed in his child through discipline, not to make the child happy.

So how do we know what's good for us? We start by getting to know God's goodness better. When we do, we will find that God's goodness demands more from us than just the kindness and tolerance that we would naturally prefer. God's goodness desires to make us more loveable by helping rid ourselves of sin. This comes best through discipline, trials, temptations, pain, and suffering. Why? Because that is generally the time when we are the most aware of His presence.

To ask that God should just let you be is equivalent to a child asking their parent to let them do whatever they please as long as they are having fun and are happy, regardless of the consequences. In this scenario, a parent would have to stop being a loving parent in the same way that God should cease being a loving God.

It seems like a paradox to say that God loves you more than anyone is this world, so much so that He would come in physical form to this earth and die for you, yet at the same time to say that God does not need you. The fact is, God has no needs. If God chooses to need us, it's because we need to be needed. He loves and needs us for our sake, not His own.

God knows that we are most content when we find our happiness in Him, not ourselves. When we want something other than what God wants for us, we will not be happy. God demands our worship, our obedience, and all of our energy and strength even though He does not need it and His glory will not be diminished if we do not. But if we do not, it only proves that we have not accepted the love of God yet.

# Chapter 4

We've come to understand that God is powerful and good. His goodness desires to make us lovable, which involves breaking us of our wicked nature in order to heal us. But this begs the question, aren't I already good and already lovable? How could I be an undeserving being? What have I ever done to God?

The problem with the human race is that, over time, we have come to believe that we are without any character defects. We believe that for the most part, we are good and that virtue alone is sufficient for a relationship with God. In addition, we have convinced ourselves that vices like cowardice, falsehood, and envy are just natural and that we need to condition ourselves to overcome the guilt associated with them.

Yet despite our best efforts to live out this virtuous standard, we are, at the core, still wicked. Since God cannot love us while we are in this wicked state, He uses pain and suffering to clean us up so He can fully love us.

The problem continues to worsen as culture progresses and the call for Christian repentance and conversion in largely unintelligible. In fact, we have created various nuances in an attempt to pass off guilt and justify our behavior, including:

- Comparing ourselves to others.
- Placing more emphasis on corporate guilt by precluding individual guilt.
- Imagining wrongly that time cancels sins.
- Believing our sinful actions must be okay if "everyone is doing it."
- Comparing our culture to others from the past.
- Diminishing all virtues down to kindness.
- Complaining that God's rules are too moralistic.
- Shifting the blame of our sin and temptation onto God.

We no longer see ourselves as sinners but rather victims who tend to transfer responsibility of our sin to something or someone, usually God, in a vain attempt to prevent personal culpability.

Fortunately for us, God's love is compatible with the pain and suffering that sin causes, and He will not rest until He sees us healed. This is in light of the fact that all of our sin is ultimately against Him! Understanding it from that perspective, we begin to see that all of our pain and suffering caused by sin is merely a direct connection to the goodness, grace, and mercy of God.

We must reclaim conviction, redemption, and an understanding of original sin if we are to ever truly appreciate the grace of God and His love for us.

# Chapter 5

A skeptic may question why a good and loving God would create evil human beings.

The good news is that He didn't. In fact, in the creation story, God created us in His perfect and good image with a free will that was to be used to honor and love Him. The bad news is that we took that free will and used it to make war on our Creator, believing that we could be our own god. This abuse of our freedom made us the abominable, wicked creatures that we are now and is what is referred to at the doctrine of the Fall.

Some say that modern science and philosophies disprove this doctrine and that the human race has made advancements and refinements and slowly risen out of brutality and savagery. Regarding science, Lewis has no objection to the idea that people physically descended from animals but rejects the idea that the further back you go in time, the more wicked and wretched you will find man to be.

Regarding philosophy, he claims that our prehistoric ancestors weren't as unsophisticated as we make them out to be. They made all the useful discoveries, like that of language, family, clothing, fire, domestication of animals, the wheel, the ship, poetry, and agriculture. Therefore, Lewis claims that science has nothing to say for or against the doctrine of the Fall.

Having put to rest any scientific controversy, Lewis now moves on to his own interpretation of the story of creation and the Fall. Lewis summarizes that over centuries, God perfected the animal form that was eventually to become human. Once perfected, He gave it a consciousness or awareness of itself as well as of God, and it had the responsibility of commanding all other lower life forms. Every thought the human had of God was of obedient love, worship, and joy. He was the prototype of Christ. We are not sure how many of these creatures God created, but sooner or later, they decided that they could be as gods and could call their souls their own. This act of self-will against our Creator is what led to the Fall of man.

Before the Fall, the human spirit obeyed and loved God without painful effort and had full control over its consciousness, intellect, emotions, fears, passions, and creativity, not to mention possessing a free will—a gift that no other creature had. After the Fall, the human spirit, having cut itself off from the source of its power, was now damaged. The control the human spirit once had over its body now ceased and is now characterized as spiritually "dead" and in rebellion to God.

Lewis said that once the human spirit began to revolt, God began to rule the creature not by the laws of the spirit but by those of nature. The organs, no longer governed by man's will, fell under the control of ordinary biochemical laws and suffered whatever the inter-workings of those laws might bring about in the way of pain, senility, and death. The will, caught in the tidal wave of mere nature, had no resource but to force back some of the new thoughts and desires, and these became the subconscious as we now know it.

When Adam sinned, he did not die physically that day, but he died spiritually. Ever since, the human spirit has borne the effects of the Fall, which include pain and suffering.


# Chapter 6

When experiencing pain, where do most people go in this generation to find answers? My guess is Google. Google has become the god of this age that provides at least one million searchable results all claiming to have the perfect solution to fix our pain—or sometimes convince us there is no hope for our pain at all. It all depends on the luck of the search that day.

Instead, we should go to the only one who does not necessarily promise to take away the pain but rather to give us rest. The only catch is, well, more pain. This new pain involves surrendering your self-will (your own desires and ideas) and thereby trusting in His. You might even have to experience spiritual death.

Here's how it works. Over time, your human spirit has become hardened, living contently and comfortably in an illusion that says all is well. As a Christ follower, you might even acknowledge the idea of self-surrender and think you are actually living it.

Then something happens that causes you pain and suffering, and your comfortable illusion is shattered. As the pain gets worse, it becomes apparent that you simply do not possess the ability or resources to stop the pain. You finally submit your will to God's as your one and only last option. God, who has no pride, scoops you up and, over time, provides rest, direction, wisdom, and, many times, deliverance from the pain. Then, once the disaster has been alleviated or averted, the human spirit takes over again and returns you to your happy illusion, all waiting on the next painful event.

How do we change this cycle in our lives? Our desires must be changed from pleasing self to pleasing God, which, in the end, produces our greatest happiness. We must lose ourselves to find ourselves truly satisfied in God.

Lewis asserts that pain is God's tool to nudge us toward our ultimate aim in life: self-surrender by putting God's will above our own. When we do this, we will no longer live in illusions of happiness but rather experience true happiness grounded in imitating Christ in this life with a confident hope of heaven in the afterlife.

# Chapter 7

It has been said that the Beatitudes found in Jesus's Sermon on the Mount are the "attitudes that one should be." But when we look at the Beatitudes, quite a few of these propositions sound like they could cause some unhappiness, at least in the worldly sense of the word: "Blessed are they who mourn," "Blessed are they who are persecuted," etc. These afflictions hardly seem to suggest a recipe for pleasant emotions.

Jesus never promised us a Christian life void of pain. On the contrary, He said that in this world we would experience suffering, but as we suffer, we will be blessed. So does that mean we should pursue suffering? No, but when suffering is experienced through the natural stages of life, we must submit that pain to God and allow Him to lead us through it. In addition, our awareness of our own pain should make us compassionate toward others when they are afflicted.

This compassion for others will often lead us to rout out suffering through social and economic reforms and perhaps even through political and governmental authorities. Unfortunately, this is a self-defeating proposition as suffering will not cease until God sees the world as redeemed or as beyond redemption. It's not that we shouldn't seek drastic changes to improve the sufferer's plight, but it's the Christian's obligation to serve others in that capacity, not the government's, as we have the unique relationship with God. Government is man's creation, and it will ultimately serve him and not God.

Through our suffering, it might seem as though God is withholding happiness because He certainly has the power to provide it. However, the happiness and security we crave would teach us to rest our hearts in this world and thereby create obstacles to our reliance on God. God will certainly provide joy and pleasures in this life but never settled happiness or security lest we try to make this world our home.

We must also be careful when we speak of suffering as cumulative in that we actually make the problem of pain worse. All suffering is uniquely personal and not cumulative. There is no such thing as a sum of suffering. You can no more experience another's suffering than you can their exhaustion from a good day's work. There is only one who experienced cumulative suffering, and He did so on the cross for all of humanity.

Finally, as sin tends to proliferate and spread, pain does not. It's not contagious. When it's over, it's over, and the natural result is joy. This joy is deeper than a mere emotional state as it is rooted in Christ's promise of salvation—a promise that sees us through the pain and suffering we experience here on Earth.

# Chapter 8

How can a loving God send people to hell? The good news is, He doesn't. The bad news is, we send ourselves there.

Given the option, why would anyone choose hell? The reason people finally go to hell is because they do not desire God, and God will not force us to desire Him, because doing so would violate our free will. He does intervene in our lives however, often through earthly pain, to try to redeem us, yet many refuse.

The idea of hell is so appalling that many outright object to it for a variety of reasons, including the idea that dispensing punishment for bad behavior is unjust. But how can God be unjust when He refuses forgiveness to those who never repent and who desire to remain what they are— sinful? Isn't He giving them exactly what they desire—separation from Him? God will not violate our free will; rather, He honors it even to our detriment.

One might also object to the huge gap between sins in an average lifetime compared to an eternity of punishment. In other words, if we just had a little more time and were given a few more chances, we would repent. God would give a million chances if it were likely to do any good. Finality must come sometime. Omniscience knows when.

Others might also object to the scary and intense symbolism used to describe hell. The symbols of hell are grotesque for a reason. They are meant to point to realities that are far worse.

We might also object to the thought of the residents of heaven grieving over their loved ones in hell being punished. Although we may not have a complete understanding, we do know that hell has no power over heaven. In heaven, we will have a new perspective void of any sadness, grief, or darkness. Perhaps we will have no knowledge or remembrance of those loved ones at all.

Lastly, we might object on the grounds that God is not all-powerful if just one lost soul ends up in hell. This isn't an objection but a reality. God is all-powerful yet provided His creation a free will that they used to reject Him. "The doors of Hell are locked from the inside out." It's not the angry wrath of God giving sinners what they deserve. Hell is a place of self-exile.

We might find it easier to think of hell as simply separation from God that is an inescapable byproduct of our free will. However horrible the conditions of hell actually are, they will never sway those who refuse to repent no matter how many chances are offered.

# Chapter 9

One of life's greatest joys is having a pet. They bring so much happiness, companionship, and enjoyment that we can't imagine life without them. As a result, we tend to apply an almost human-like quality to our pets, and it comforts us to think they are in a better place, free of suffering, when they die.

And why shouldn't we? We know that animals possess intelligence and the ability to care. Various animals seem to be able to communicate with other members of their species. Dogs can be trained to do almost anything, and monkeys, gorillas, and chimpanzees have been taught sign language.

But does animal intelligence constitute an immortal spirit that will survive after death? Scripture never tells us specifically what happens to animals after death or if their pain and suffering have any redemptive purpose. God has given us some means of coming to terms with our own suffering as it ultimately leads to redemption, but with animals, we have no such knowledge.

We are left to wonder if animals have the same awareness of pain and suffering as we do. If so, how did pain enter the animal world, and how will God make things right in the end?

Because of what we do know about our own suffering and the goodness of God, we can be confident that animal pain is not the result of cruelty on the part of God. We can also understand that animals lack a consciousness (or awareness), so they cannot experience and realize the fact of their pain. Animals may have pain but can never experience suffering and the ability to reflect upon that pain.

Unfortunately, God has not seen fit to reveal to us a true understanding of animal pain and the role that suffering might play in an animal's life. Everything that humans think they know about animal pain is really only guesswork.

## Chapter 10

When experiencing pain and suffering brought about by the struggles of life, we must have hope. This hope cannot be based on anything in this world, because this world is failing. Our hope must be based on our faith and trust in Jesus Christ and the forgiveness that He offers to those who believe. Ultimately, this hope manifests itself after death in the form of heaven, where we will be found eternally living in the presence of God without pain and without suffering.

To some, heaven might appear to be a placebo for the weak to help ease the burdens of life. However, Lewis speculates that heaven is actually the fulfillment of the deepest desires of all humanity. We might think of these desires in terms of those secret longings that give us partial joy on Earth but somehow keep us yearning in our hearts for something more—something unnamable that we just cannot explain. This something is heaven.

Whereas hell is the separation from all that is holy, heaven was made to uniquely satisfy our deepest longings and affections while living in the presence of God.

Pain is never pointless, and God never abandons us in the midst of suffering. He will do whatever it takes to communicate with His people and guide them in the path He has planned. This path often includes pain. However, a believer understands that all suffering and pain will make sense in light of eternity. This is the hope that we have—hope of the ultimate reward for suffering in this world: heaven.

# QUOTES

All of C.S. Lewis's writings are extremely quotable. In fact, if you search the web, you will find plenty of them, including websites, Facebook pages, and Twitter feeds dedicated to the task. On the next several pages, you will find some of my favorite quotes from *The Problem of Pain.* I'm sure you have your own!

## PREFACE

"…when pain is to be born, a little courage helps more than much knowledge, a little human sympathy more than much courage, and the least tincture of the love of God more than all."

## INTRODUCTORY

"All men alike stand condemned, not by alien codes of ethics, but by their own, and all men therefore are conscious of guilt. [Moral consciousness] is either inexplicable illusion, or else revelation."

## DIVINE OMNIPOTENCE

"Try to exclude the possibility of suffering which the order of nature and the existence of free-wills involve, and you find that you have excluded life itself."

## DIVINE GOODNESS

"I do not think I should value much the love of a friend who cared only for my happiness and did not object to my becoming dishonest."

"A man can no more diminish God's glory by refusing to worship Him than a lunatic can put out the sun by scribbling the word 'darkness' on the walls of his cell."

"To be God—to be like God and to share His goodness in creaturely response—to be miserable—these are the only three alternatives. If we will not learn to eat the only food that the universe grows—the only food that any possible universe can ever grow—then we must starve eternally."

"Love may forgive all infirmities and love still in spite of them: but Love cannot cease to will their removal."

"Love may, indeed, love the beloved when her beauty is lost: but not because it is lost. Love may forgive all infirmities and love still in spite of them: but Love cannot cease to will their removal. Love is more sensitive than hatred itself to every blemish in the beloved… Of all powers he forgives most, but he condones least: he is pleased with little, but demands all."

"Love, in its own nature, demands the perfecting of the beloved."

"We want not so much a Father but a grandfather in heaven, a God who said of anything we happened to like doing, 'What does it matter so long as they are contented?'"

## HUMAN WICKEDNESS

"God may be more than moral goodness: He is not less. The road to the promised land runs past Sinai. The moral law may exist to be transcended: but there is no transcending it for those who have not first admitted its claims upon them, and then tried with all their strength to meet that claim, and fairly and squarely faced the fact of their failure."

"Everyone feels benevolent if nothing happens to be annoying him at the moment."

## HUMAN PAIN

"No doubt Pain as God's megaphone is a terrible instrument; it may lead to final and unrepentant rebellion. But it gives the only opportunity the bad man can have for amendment. It removes the veil; it plants the flag of truth within the fortress of the rebel soul."

"Prostitutes are in no danger of finding their present life so satisfactory that they cannot turn to God: the proud, the avaricious, the self-righteous, are in that danger."

"We can ignore even pleasure. But pain insists upon being attended to. God whispers to us in our pleasures, speaks in our conscience, but shouts in our pains: it is his megaphone to rouse a deaf world."

"Pain is unmasked, unmistakable evil; every man knows that something is wrong when he is being hurt."

"We regard God as an airman regards his parachute; it's there for emergencies but he hopes he'll never have to use it."

"Our Father refreshes us on the journey with some pleasant inns, but will not encourage us to mistake them for home."

"If tribulation is a necessary element in redemption, we must anticipate that it will never cease till God sees the world to be either redeemed or no further redeemable."

## HUMAN PAIN CONTINUED

"For you will certainly carry out God's purpose, however you act, but it makes a difference to you whether you serve like Judas or like John."

## HELL

"In the long run the answer to all those who object to the doctrine of hell is itself a question: 'What are you asking God to do?' To wipe out their past sins and, at all costs, to give them a fresh start, smoothing every difficulty and offering every miraculous help? But He has done so, on Calvary. To forgive them? They will not be forgiven. To leave them alone? Alas, I am afraid that is what He does."

"To enter heaven is to become more human than you ever succeeded in being on earth; to enter hell, is to be banished from humanity."

## HEAVEN

Your place in heaven will seem to be made for you and you alone, because you were made for it—made for it stitch by stitch as a glove is made for a hand."

"It is safe to tell the pure in heart that they shall see God, for only the pure in heart want to."

# MERE CHRISTIANITY STUDY GUIDE

A Bible Study on the C.S. Lewis Book *Mere Christianity*

By Steven Urban

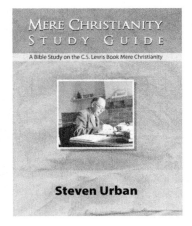

*Mere Christianity Study Guide* takes participants through a study of C.S. Lewis's classic *Mere Christianity*. Yet despite its recognition as a "classic," there is surprisingly little available today in terms of a serious study course.

This 12-week Bible study digs deep into each chapter and, in turn, into Lewis's thoughts. Perfect for small group sessions, this interactive workbook includes daily, individual study as well as a complete appendix and commentary to supplement and further clarify certain topics. Multiple week format options are also included.

## WHAT OTHERS ARE SAYING:

*This study guide is more than just a guide to C.S Lewis' Mere Christianity, it is a guide to Christianity itself.* – Crystal

*Wow! What a lot of insight and food for thought! Perfect supplement to Mere Christianity. I think Mr. Lewis himself would approve.* – Laurie

*Our group is in the middle of studying Mere Christianity and I have found this guide to be invaluable.* – Angela

*This is a very useful and comprehensive guide to Mere Christianity.* – John

To learn more about Mere Christianity Study Guide or to find retailers please visit
## www.BrownChairBooks.com

# FOREWARD

During World War II, C. S. Lewis delivered a series of radio broadcasts on the BBC in England. At the time of the broadcasts the outcome of the war was still very uncertain. People needed hope. Many tuned in to see what this Oxford scholar might have to say. Later the talks were published as the book *Mere Christianity*. Since its publication thousands of thoughtful people have found their way to a faith in Christ that makes sense. Included among these is Dr. Francis Collins, the scientist who broke the Genome, and also Charles Colson, President Nixon's chief of staff, and later founder of Prison Fellowship. *Mere Christianity* is for the thinking person. But the book appeals to the heart as well. In fact, it appeals to the whole person. It is not a surprise that this should be so.

In his literary criticism of his friend and fellow Inkling, Charles Williams' Arthurian Poems, *The Arthurian Torso*, C. S. Lewis said, "The first problem in life is how do you fit the stone [the Reason] and the shell [the Romantic longings of the heart]?" Lewis himself came to believe that Christianity did this best. In fact, after his long spell as an atheist, Lewis's first Christian book was titled, *The Pilgrim's Regress: An Allegorical Apology for Christianity, Reason and Romanticism*. He wrote to show that Christianity was a holistic faith that reconciled head and heart. This is because faith in Christ is a reconciling faith. It reconciles those estranged from God into a robust relationship with God. It gives the resources to make possible reconciliation of broken relationships with others. In fact, it provides the means to repair the ruins within one's own life. It sets the believer on the course of reconciling the soul and body as well as the head and the heart.

Lewis is known for his ability to open wardrobe doors into magical worlds where the themes of reconciliation are made accessible through children's stories like the Narnian Chronicles; written for children but very readable for adults. So too, one is grateful when someone comes along and opens a wardrobe door into an enriched understanding of Lewis's books.

This is what one encounters in Dr. Steven Urban's *Mere Christianity Study Guide: A Bible Study on the C. S. Lewis Book Mere Christianity*. With all of the diagnostic skill of a physician, Urban offers fresh insight on this Christian Classic making Lewis's thought all the more accessible for those who long to better understand Lewis and his ideas. Urban makes the book come alive with valuable applications for spiritual growth and maturity. In fact the book could be titled: C. S. Lewis's Spiritual Formation for Mere Christians. Urban is right to suggest that Lewis's book is not merely a work in Christian Apologetics and defense of the faith. Its themes are far richer than that. Lewis is concerned not only that the faith is defensible but it is also transformational. This fact is certainly developed by Dr. Urban.

Urban developed this study of *Mere Christianity* while teaching an adult Sunday school class. Over some time he developed the curriculum. Now, his treatment of *Mere Christianity* provides a valuable resource for the Church at large. All over the world Christians have studied *Mere Christianity* in Sunday schools and small groups around the globe. But never has such an in-depth study of the book been developed and made transferable for others to use while teaching from this classic text.

Urban has served well all who want such an aid to enhance their own teaching. I have been studying C. S. Lewis for 44 years. I have taught Lewis courses and lectured about Lewis for 34 years at 58 university campuses in 11 different countries around the world. Urban's study of Mere Christianity is the best I've seen.

It pleases me to see he is making his own study of Lewis available to others. You see, I've known Steve for over 35 years. My own grasp of Lewis was deeply influenced by things I learned from Steve while I was still in graduate school. It is high time others can have the privilege of gaining from his many years study of Lewis. I recommend the book for all who take their faith seriously and want to grow to be all they can be in Christ.

Jerry Root, PhD
Editor of *The Quotable C.S. Lewis*
Consulting Editor of *The C.S. Lewis Study Bible*

# BOOK 1

## RIGHT AND WRONG AS A CLUE TO THE MEANING OF THE UNIVERSE

## CHAPTER 1: THE LAW OF HUMAN NATURE

1.  What is it that we can learn from people disagreeing or quarreling? (para. 1-2)

2.  What are some of the different names Lewis says this can or has been called? (para. 3)

3.  How is the Law of Human Nature different from other laws of nature? (para. 3-4)

4.  Why in the past have people called this Rule about Right and Wrong the Law of Nature? (para. 5)

5.  On what basis have some denied that the Law of (Human) Nature is known to all men? (para. 6)

6.     How does Lewis respond to this denial? (para. 7-8)

7.     Agreeing that Right and Wrong are *real or objective* and not merely a matter of taste, preference or opinion, what is the next point Lewis makes about our human Law of Nature? (para. 9-10)

8.     Put Lewis's final summary into your own words: (para. 11)

# THE SCREWTAPE LETTERS STUDY GUIDE

A Bible Study on the C.S. Lewis Book *The Screwtape Letters*

By Alan Vermilye

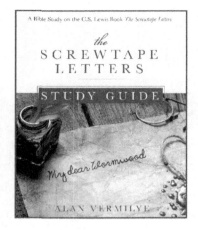

*The Screwtape Letters Study Guide* takes participants through a study of C.S. Lewis's classic, *The Screwtape Letters*.

This Bible study digs deep into each letter from Screwtape, an undersecretary in the lowerarchy of Hell, to his incompetent nephew Wormwood a junior devil. Perfect for small group sessions this interactive workbook includes daily, individual study with a complete answer guide available online.

Designed as a 12-week study, multiple week format options are also included.

## WHAT OTHERS ARE SAYING:

*This book and study creates a positive reinforcement on fighting that Spiritual battle in life. Great read, great study guide!* – Lester

*This study guide was a wonderful way for our group to work through the Screwtape Letters!* - Becky

*Use this Study Guide for a Fresh "Seeing" of the Screwtape Letters!* – William

*This is an essential companion if you are reading The Screwtape Letters as a small group.* – J.T.

To learn more about The Screwtape Letters Study Guide or to find retailers please visit
## www.BrownChairBooks.com

# INTRODUCTION

For some time I wanted to read *The Screwtape Letters*. I would start, and then, for whatever reason, stop. Let's face it: some of Lewis' writings can be an intellectual exercise that require dedication to seeing them through. I would say this is especially true for me. However, having read his *Mere Christianity* several times and completing the *Mere Christianity Study Guide* by Steve Urban twice, I felt I was finally up to the challenge.

I committed myself to both reading the book and creating a Bible study guide for it. Recognizing the daunting task before me, I decided to lead the study at my own church while writing it. I knew this would help develop the study and provide the accountability I would desperately need to see it through.

*The Screwtape Letters* is not a very long book. There are 31 letters that are only five pages each and at the most six paragraphs. I began with research and found some insightful posts, commentaries, and a few discussion questions to help prime the pump. I also kept Google handy since Lewis was a very articulate man with a vast vocabulary.

Creating a Bible study around the content seemed to flow effortlessly. Obviously Lewis already provided excellent content; I simply had to draw parallels with various Scripture passages to help us relate to the main theme of each letter. I have also included answers for each question that are available at www.ScrewtapeLettersStudyGuide.com.

Facilitating group discussion at my church was probably the most valuable part of the experience. Not only did it help better refine the study, but I also learned from each class member as they shared their interpretation of what they read. I'm eternally grateful for their participation and input on the study.

# LETTER 1
## REASON AND REALITY

## Summary

In this letter, we learn that Wormwood has been making sure that his patient spends plenty of time with his materialistic friends. Wormwood believes that by using reason and argument he can keep the man from belief in God. Screwtape does not disagree that it is good to influence the man's thoughts, but he reminds Wormwood that his main job is to keep the patient from thinking too deeply about any spiritual matter. Instead he should use ordinary everyday distraction to mislead the man.

> *The trouble about argument is that it moves the whole struggle onto the Enemy's own ground.* - Screwtape

## Discussion Questions

1. In what way does Screwtape say that Wormwood is being naive? ¶ 1

2. What is Screwtape's explanation of why Wormwood should avoid reliance on "argument"? ¶ 2

3. What is the connection between "thinking and doing", and how does this impact our daily lives? ¶ 1

4. Screwtape claims that people "having a dozen incompatible philosophies dancing together inside their head". What specifically does he credit for this? What do you think the other "weapons" are today? How can they be used to destroy argument? ¶ 1

5. If, according to Screwtape, people are not persuaded by what is true or false, what does he say people are concerned with? Why do people believe what they believe? ¶ 1

6. Read Hebrews 2:14-18. What is the "abominable advantage" God has over Satan? How should this encourage us in our Christian walk? ¶ 3

7. The story of the atheist in the British museum provides a dark and somewhat disturbing insight into rather pleasant distractions that can draw us away from spiritual matters. In this particular instance, the atheist's appetite was enough to pull him away from his train of thought in which God was working. How can Satan use common distractions to create detours in the course of our daily lives? ¶ 3

8. Why would Screwtape advise Wormwood to "Keep pressing home on him the *ordinariness* of things."? What "comfort zones" in our Christian walk do we need to be cautious of? ¶ 4

9. Read Luke 10:39-42. What ordinary everyday distractions was Martha concerned with? Who did it make her resent? What did she miss out on?

# THE GREAT DIVORCE STUDY GUIDE

A Bible Study on the C.S. Lewis Book *The Great Divorce*

By Alan Vermilye

*The Great Divorce Study Guide* is an 8-week Bible study on the C.S. Lewis classic, The Great Divorce. Perfect for small groups or individual study, each weekly study session applies a biblical framework to the concepts found in each chapter of the book. Although intriguing and entertaining, much of Lewis's writings can be difficult to grasp.

*The Great Divorce Study Guide* will guide you through each one of Lewis' masterful metaphors to a better understanding of the key concepts of the book, the supporting Bible passages, and the relevance to our world today. Each study question is ideal for group discussion and answers to each question are available online.

## WHAT OTHERS ARE SAYING:

*To my knowledge, there have not been many study guides for either of these so to see this new one on "The Great Divorce" (both electronic and print) is a welcome sight!* – Richard

*I recommend the Great Divorce Study Guide to anyone or any group wishing to delve more deeply into the question, why would anyone choose hell over heaven!* - Ruth

*The questions were thought-provoking, and I very much liked how everything was evaluated by scripture. Would definitely recommend!* – Justin

*I can't imagine studying C.S. Lewis' book without this study guide. We will use Vermilye's other guides in the future.* – Jim

To learn more about The Great Divorce Study Guide or to find retailers please visit

## www.BrownChairBooks.com

# INTRODUCTION

What is the most desirable place you can think of to take a vacation? Perhaps it is a place that you have been before or someplace you dream of going. How would you respond if, once you arrived, you were invited to stay on this vacation forever? However, in order to stay, you must leave your old life behind. You cannot go back and say goodbye or set your affairs in order. You either must commit at that moment or return to your previous life.

How hard would it be for you to leave behind the life you are now living? It might be an easy decision for some and much more difficult for others.

In *The Great Divorce* by C.S. Lewis, damned spirits are given a vacation or a "holiday" away from Hell to visit Heaven, where they are invited to stay forever. There, they are persuaded by people they formally knew, relatives and friends, to come with them up the mountain to enjoy the bliss of Heaven. But they can only do so by leaving behind what is keeping them in Hell and accepting the love of God.

The answer seems obvious, right? Yet what we'll find is that it's not the choice to sin that binds people to Hell but rather the choice not to repent. We must let go, step out into the light, and embrace the better life that God has planned for us. That's the most confining part about sin—to admit you're in the wrong.

Lewis tells us not to take this story literally, nor does he suppose that eternity really is the way he presents it in the book. The fact is, Hell is final. Scripture records no opportunities offered after death to enter Heaven. On the title page of your book by Lewis, there is a telling quote from George MacDonald: "No, there is no escape. There is no heaven with a little of hell in it—no plan to retain this or that of the devil in our hearts or our pockets. Out Satan must go, every hair and feather."

In this story, Lewis quite vividly illustrates for us that we are all soul searching and our efforts either move us toward or away from God. It's a progression away from our own idea of what we think is best for us toward the humility required to embrace God's best for our lives. It can be painful to leave our old life behind, but with each step, it gets a little easier, and any pain will be nothing compared to the joy we will experience in Heaven.

I thoroughly enjoyed putting together this Bible study. As with all my studies, I write them for the small groups that I facilitate at my own church. Not only does it help better refine the study but I also learn from each class member as they share their interpretation of what they read. I'm eternally grateful for their participation and input on the study.

# CHAPTER 1:
# THE NATURE OF HELL

As the story begins, Lewis, also our narrator, finds himself waiting in a long line for a magical bus ride in a dismally uncomforting grey town. His companions in line are argumentative, combative, and generally disagreeable and of differing economic and educational backgrounds. As the story progresses we learn that these characters are damned souls on vacation, and that the grey town is Purgatory for some and the outskirts of Hell for others.

> *Why on earth they insist on coming I can't imagine. They won't like it at all when we get there, and they'd really be much more comfortable at home.*

## Discussion Questions

1. Describe in detail the mood, atmosphere, images, and depictions of the grey town. Do you find Lewis's depiction of Hell or Purgatory "accurate"?

2. Although the grey town is revealed within the contexts of the story to be the outer limits of Hell, or Purgatory for those who will eventually reach Heaven, the reader is to consider this an imaginative representation of Hell rather than an accurate, biblical representation of the real Hell. Using the following Bible passages, describe the nature of Hell. In your own words, how would you describe Hell to a friend?

    a) Revelation 14:10–11  –
    b) 2 Thessalonians 1:9 –
    c) Revelation 21:8 –
    d) Matthew 25:41 –
    e) Mark 9:44–49 –
    f) Revelation 20:10 –
    g) Matthew 13:41–42 –
    h) Matthew 3:12 –
    i) Daniel 12:2 –
    j) Luke 16:23–24 –

3. The souls that Lewis encounters while waiting for and getting on the bus seem to represent various forms of sin in what used to be called the capital sins or what is commonly referred to as the seven deadly sins. Associate the different personalities he encounters in line and on the bus with the appropriate sin below.

    a) Envy – the desire to have an item, an experience, or feeling that someone else possesses
    b) Gluttony – an excessive, ongoing consumption of food or drink
    c) Greed – an excessive pursuit of material possessions
    d) Lust – an uncontrollable passion or longing, especially for sexual desires
    e) Vanity or Pride – excessive view of one's self without regard to others
    f) Sloth – excessive laziness or the failure to act and utilize one's talents
    g) Wrath or Anger – uncontrollable feelings of anger and hate toward another person

4. As people continue to leave the bus line, what principle is Lewis trying to establish regarding a town in which any real life is absent yet there is little desire to move beyond it?

5. The souls complain about the bus driver, saying, "Why can't he behave naturally?" Read 1 Corinthians 2:14. Why do unbelievers have difficulty relating to or understanding a believer's joy?

6. The tousle-haired poet cannot imagine why the other souls would insist on coming on the bus and concludes that they would be much more comfortable at home. What parallel is there to our comfort and how we deal with sin? Read 1 John 1:8 and Romans 12:9. How do we break free of that sin comfort zone?

7. What do you think of Lewis's idea that there will be fish and chips and movies and advertising in Hell?

# THE SCREWTAPE LETTERS STUDY GUIDE FOR TEENS

A Bible Study for Teenagers on the C.S. Lewis Book *The Screwtape Letters*

By Alan Vermilye

*The Screwtape Letters Study Guide for Teens* takes teenagers through a study of the C.S. Lewis classic, *The Screwtape Letters*.

Created specifically for teenagers, each daily study is designed to take them through each letter written by Screwtape, an undersecretary in the lowerarchy of Hell, to his incompetent nephew Wormwood, a junior devil.

The interactive workbook is perfect for individual study or group study to include youth groups, homeschool groups, or small groups.

# SCREWTAPE PROPOSES A TOAST STUDY GUIDE

A Bible Study on the C.S. Lewis Essay *Screwtape Proposes a Toast*

By Alan Vermilye

Only the imaginative mind of C.S. Lewis could create a short story about a demon offering the after-dinner speech at the graduation ceremony at the Tempters' Training College for young demons.

Nearly two decades after the release of *The Screwtape Letters* and to the delight of his fans, Lewis wrote a sequel that he never intended to create. In fact, he never imagined the original book would become a classic and that his readers would continue to enjoy it so many years later.

*Screwtape Proposes a Toast Study Guide* digs deep into this classic and provides a Bible study for individual use or small groups. This flexible study can be used in one long setting or divided up over several sessions.

To learn more about either of these books or to find retailers please visit
## www.BrownChairBooks.com

# THE 90-DAY BIBLE STUDY GUIDE

A Bible Study Tour of the Greatest Story Ever Told

By Bruce Gust

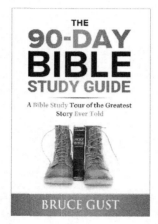

*The 90-Day Bible Study* Guide takes you on a journey through select portions of Scripture covering a survey of the Bible in just 90 days! The perfect Bible study for beginners, bible study for teens, homeschool groups, adult Bible studies, or those seasoned veterans looking for a refresher Bible study course.

Beginning with Genesis and ending in Revelations, you'll spend just under 30 minutes each day in this Bible Study Guide and workbook on Scripture readings and corresponding Bible study questions designed to guide you to a better understanding of the personalities, the history, the conflicts, the miracles and the Truth that is the Christian faith.

## WHAT OTHERS ARE SAYING:

*Bruce Gust takes us back to the basics with easy to digest truths and thought provoking questions!*
– Russell

*This study guide seeks to challenge you to find out the truth from God's word by reading the Bible.*
- Stephen

*A great way to dig into various parts of Scripture, all the while getting a bigger picture of the overall Story of the Bible.* - Allie

*Simple, informative and it highlights the main storyline in the Bible, redemption. Well done!* – Jim

To learn more about The 90-Day Bible Study Guide or to find retailers please visit
## www.BrownChairBooks.com